Handling Difficult People and Situations

Lead people through adversity

Rick Conlow
Doug Watsabaugh

A Crisp Fifty-Minute™ Series Book

AXZO PRESS

Handling Difficult People and Situations

Lead people through adversity

Rick Conlow
Doug Watsabaugh

CREDITS:

President, Axzo Press:	**Jon Winder**
Vice President, Product Development:	**Charles G. Blum**
Vice President, Operations:	**Josh Pincus**
Director, Publishing Systems Development:	**Dan Quackenbush**
Copy Editor:	**Catherine M. Albano**

Trademarks

Crisp Fifty-Minute Series is a trademark of Axzo Press.

Some of the product names and company names used in this book have been used for identification purposes only and may be trademarks or registered trademarks of their respective manufacturers and sellers.

Disclaimer

We reserve the right to revise this publication and make changes from time to time in its content without notice.

ISBN 10: 1-4260-1844-4
ISBN 13: 978-1-4260-1844-2

Printed in the United States of America

1 2 3 4 5 08 07 06

Table of Contents

About the Author

Rick Conlow

A quick glance at his professional resume leaves you with the strong impression that effort and optimism are a winning combination. Case in point: With Rick by their side, clients have achieved double- and triple-digit improvement in their sales performance, quality, customer loyalty, and service results over the past 20-plus years and earned more than 30 quality and service awards.

In an age where optimism and going the extra mile can sound trite, Rick has made them a differentiator. His clients include organizations that lead their industries, as well as others that are less recognizable. Regardless, their goals are his goals.

Rick's life view and extensive background in sales and leadership—as a general manager, vice president, training director, program director, national sales trainer, and consultant—are the foundation of his coaching, training, and consulting services. Participants in Rick's experiential, "live action" programs walk away with ah-has, inspiration, and skills they can immediately put to use.

These programs include:

- ▶ BEST Selling!
- ▶ Moments of Magic!
- ▶ Excellence in Management!
- ▶ SuperSTAR Service and Selling!
- ▶ The Greatest Secrets of all Time!
- ▶ Good Boss/Bad Boss—Which One Are You?

Rick has also authored *Excellence in Management, Excellence in Supervision, Returning to Learning,* and *Moments of Magic.*

When he's not engaging an audience or engrossed in a coaching discussion, this proud husband and father is most likely astride a weight bench or on a motorcycle taking on the back roads and highways of Minnesota.

Doug Watsabaugh

Doug values being a "regular person," with his feet on the ground and head in the realities of the daily challenges his clients face. It's his heart for and experience in helping clients deal with difficult situations that distinguish him from other sales performance and leadership development consultants.

His knowledge of experiential learning and his skill at designing change processes and learning events have enabled him to measurably improve the lives of thousands of individuals and hundreds of organizations in a wide variety of industries— financial services, manufacturing, medical devices, consumer goods, and technology, to name a few.

Before starting his own business, Doug served as the director of operations for a national training institute, manager of organization development for a major chemical company, and was responsible for worldwide training and organization development for the world's third largest toy company.

He was also a partner in Performance & Human Development LLC, a California company that published high-involvement experiential activities, surveys and instruments, interactive training modules, papers, and multimedia presentations.

Doug has co-authored two books with John E. Jones, Ph.D., and William L. Bearley, Ed. D.: *The New Fieldbook for Trainers* published by HRD Press and Lakewood Publishing, and *The OUS Quality Item Pool,* about organizational survey items that measure Baldrige criteria.

He is a member of the American Society for Training and Development (ASTD), the Minnesota Quality Council and The National Organization Development Network.

Doug's father taught him the value of hard work, and it paid dividends: He funded his college education playing guitar and singing with a rock 'n' roll band, experiencing a close call with fame when he played bass in concert with Chuck Berry. Not bad for a guy who admits to being "a bit shy."

While Doug's guitar remains a source of enjoyment, it pales in comparison to his "number one joy and priority"—his family.

WCW Partners

WCW Partners is a performance improvement company with more than 20 years of experience helping companies, governmental agencies, and nonprofit organizations worldwide revitalize their results and achieve record-breaking performance.

We are experts in sales performance, organization development, leadership development, marketing, and communications—and we don't mind telling you that we're different than most consulting firms you'll find in the marketplace.

For one thing, it's our approach—when you hire us, you get us. But just as important, we're people who've had to wrestle with the same issues you have—how to strengthen sales, boost productivity, improve quality, increase employee satisfaction, build a team, or retain and attract new customers. To us, "We develop the capability in you" is more than a catchy phrase. It's our promise.

Our clients include 3M, American Express, American Medical Systems, Amgen Inc., Accenture, AmeriPride Services, Andersen Windows, Avanade, Beltone, Canadian Linen and Uniform Service, Carew International, Case Corporation, Citigroup, Coca-Cola, Costco, Covance, Deknatel, Eaton Corporation, Electrochemicals Inc., Entergy, Esoterix, General Mills, GN Resound, Grant Thornton, Hasbro Inc., Honeywell, Interton, Kenner Products, Marketlink, Kemps-Marigold, Meijer Corporation, National Computer Systems, Parker Brothers, Toro, Productive Workplace Systems, Red Wing Shoes, Rite Aid, Rollerblade, Ryan Companies, Travelers Insurance, Thrivent, Tonka Corporation, and a number of nonprofit and educational institutions.

To learn how you can do amazing things, visit us online at WCWPartners.com or contact Doug or Rick toll free at 1-888-313-0514.

Preface

This book is about customer service. Make no mistake about it; we all face difficult people in all aspects of our customer—supplier relationships. Your customer may be a consumer who buys products from your company. Or, your customer may be another member of your organization who you work with daily and who depends on you for information or services that are necessary for the completion of a product, process, or service. Finally, your customer may be your spouse, children, or some other family member or friend with whom you are interdependent. Relating to others successfully is always a challenging and dynamic process, even when the people you are working with are well-intentioned and have strong interpersonal skills. It becomes even more challenging and complex when the people you are dealing with have goals and interests that are at "cross-purposes" with your own. And, if they are interpersonally unskilled or have developed skills that you find frustrating or challenging, it is even more difficult to maintain your composure and use the best of your skills and intentions to maintain a positive focus and strive for "customer friendly" outcomes.

In this book you will learn about yourself and about patterns of behaviors that you have encountered but haven't taken the time to understand as fully as needed. You will learn techniques and models to guide you through the minefield of "difficult people" in a productive and successful way. Strap yourself in, and get ready for a quick trip through some great information on *Handling Difficult People and Situations*!

A special note of thanks to our esteemed colleague and friend, Meg Leach, WCW Sr. Consultant, who contributed greatly to this book.

Learning Objectives

Complete this book, and you'll know how to:

1) Identify who the difficult people in your life have been in terms of their characteristics and the rewards they get for behaving as they do.

2) Examine how your personal beliefs and values play into the way you deal with difficult people. And, you'll revisit your typical first response to see if it serves you well.

3) Identify the "sources of power" your difficult people have over you, and you'll learn the degree of difficulty posed by each one.

4) Assess each difficult person to enable you to make a good decision about how to handle each situation you face.

5) Identify tools to help you find the right words, and you'll receive a process model to guide you through the interaction with uncommon grace and skill.

Workplace and Management Competencies mapping

For over 30 years, business and industry has utilized competency models to select employees. The trend to use competency-based approaches in education and training, assessment, and development of workers has experienced a more recent emergence within the Employment and Training Administration (ETA), a division of the United States Department of Labor.

The ETA's General Competency Model Framework spans a wide array of competencies from the more basic competencies, such as reading and writing, to more advanced occupation-specific competencies. The Crisp Series finds its home in what the ETA refers to as the Workplace Competencies and the Management Competencies.

Handling Difficult People and Situations covers information vital to mastering the following competencies:

Workplace Competencies:

▶ Problem Solving & Decision Making

Management Competencies:

▶ Supporting Others

▶ Clarifying Roles & Objectives

▶ Managing Conflict & Team Building

For a comprehensive mapping of Crisp Series titles to the Workplace and Management competencies, visit www.CrispSeries.com.

About the Crisp 50-Minute Series

The Crisp 50-Minute Series was designed to cover critical business and professional development topics in the shortest possible time. Our easy-to-read, easy-to-understand format can be used for self-study or for classroom training. With a wealth of hands-on exercises, the 50-Minute books keep you engaged and help you retain critical skills.

What You Need to Know

We designed the Crisp 50-Minute Series to be as self-explanatory as possible. But there are a few things you should know before you begin the book.

Exercises

Exercises look like this:

EXERCISE TITLE

Questions and other information would be here.

Keep a pencil handy. Any time you see an exercise, you should try to complete it. If the exercise has specific answers, an answer key will be provided in the appendix. (Some exercises ask you to think about your own opinions or situation; these types of exercises will not have answer keys.)

Forms

A heading like this means that the rest of the page is a form:

FORMHEAD

Forms are meant to be reusable. You might want to make a photocopy of a form before you fill it out, so that you can use it again later.

A Note to Instructors

We've tried to make the Crisp 50-Minute Series books as useful as possible as classroom training manuals. Here are some of the features we provide for instructors:

▶ PowerPoint presentations

▶ Answer keys

▶ Assessments

▶ Customization

PowerPoint Presentations

You can download a PowerPoint presentation for this book from our Web site at www.CrispSeries.com.

Answer keys

If an exercise has specific answers, an answer key will be provided in the appendix. (Some exercises ask you to think about your own opinions or situation; these types of exercises will not have answer keys.)

Assessments

For each 50-Minute Series book, we have developed a 35- to 50-item assessment. The assessment for this book is available at www.CrispSeries.com. *Assessments should not be used in any employee-selection process.*

Customization

Crisp books can be quickly and easily customized to meet your needs—from adding your logo to developing proprietary content. Crisp books are available in print and electronic form. For more information on customization, see www.CrispSeries.com.

The Difficult People in Your Life

> *You must look into other people as well as at them."*

— **Lord Chesterfield**

In this part:

▶ Who were the difficult people at various stages of your life?

▶ Recognize personality types of difficult people.

The Difficult Person in Your Life

Who have been the difficult people in your life?

It's hard to imagine anyone who has had to deal with more difficult people than Harry Potter in the series of his adventures written by J.K. Rowling. First there were the relatives with whom Harry had lived since he was a baby, the Dursleys. Uncle Vernon, Aunt Petunia, and horrible cousin Dudley made Harry live under the stairs, never celebrated his birthday, and berated him daily. Then after 11 years of being belittled, teased, and completely neglected, he finally escaped to The Hogwarts School for Wizards. Hogwarts had its own share of difficult creatures. Three-headed dogs, giants, and evil classmate Malfoy may all be reminiscent of some of the difficult people with whom you work every day. They probably came straight out of author J.K. Rowling's life experiences.

Fortunately, Harry had the option of using magic to deal with all of these nasty offenders. He could escape by making himself completely invisible or by mixing magic potions that caused one particular difficult person to throw up snakes. We, however, don't have the option of waving our wand and making bosses or neighbors disappear, or have Howler letters hurled at them.

If only it were that easy!

For the rest of us non-wizards, dealing with difficult people begins very early and there seems to be no way to avoid them. The 4-year-old difficult child in one preschool class whom everyone knew as "Hitting Jenny" became only slightly less difficult when the teachers redirected her behavior so she became "Kissing Jennny."

Grade school and high school provided their own opportunities for dealing with difficult people. There were the classmates who took your homework, friends who talked about you or excluded you from their inner circle, teachers who were unfair in their dealings with students, and, of course, parents who wouldn't let you have the privileges that all your friends had.

We survived these experiences and became adults believing we had learned how to deal with them or had surely outgrown these annoying people. But, no, the first day of our first full-time, real job, there was Annie in the next cube who talked so loudly on the phone with her friends all day that you couldn't concentrate on your work.

There was also Bill, who was the first one to speak up at every meeting but had nothing of substance to say and wouldn't stop saying it. And if co-workers weren't difficult enough, the first family reunion with your partner's family presented a whole new world of strange people with habits and history that would be completely unacceptable in your own family.

If you are very, very lucky, you can at least retreat to your own home with your generous, loving, compassionate partner and your talented, polite, and extraordinary children and pets, all of whom provide you with peace and joy! Well, maybe even in this sanctuary you will have to deal with difficult people on rare occasion.

Personal History of Difficult People in Your Life

We begin our exploration of this topic by identifying who qualifies as the difficult person in your life. Who are the people who have caused you the most discomfort at each stage of your life? What was it about them that made them so difficult?

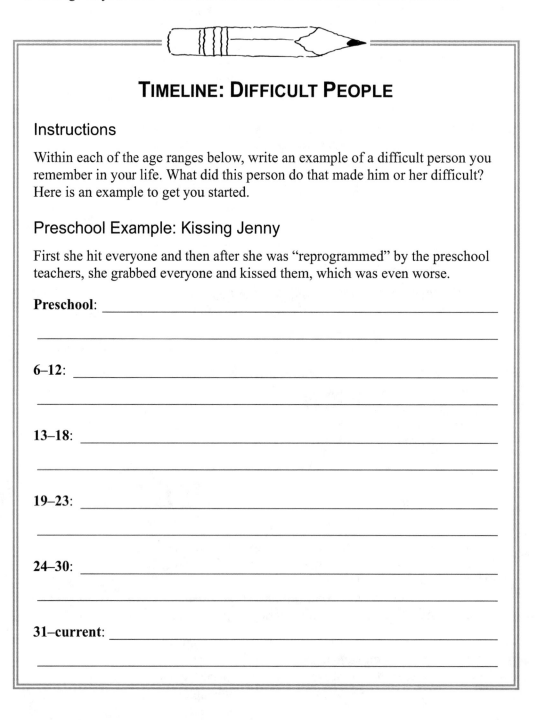

TIMELINE: DIFFICULT PEOPLE

Instructions

Within each of the age ranges below, write an example of a difficult person you remember in your life. What did this person do that made him or her difficult? Here is an example to get you started.

Preschool Example: Kissing Jenny

First she hit everyone and then after she was "reprogrammed" by the preschool teachers, she grabbed everyone and kissed them, which was even worse.

Preschool: _____

_____

6–12: _____

_____

13–18: _____

_____

19–23: _____

_____

24–30: _____

_____

31–current: _____

_____

Personality Profiles of Difficult People

As adults, we begin to see patterns of difficult people. Some are merely irritations and some are actually dangerous. These are some of the forms that difficult people can take. We'll discuss a few broad categories of personality types:

▶ Passive

▶ Indirect

▶ Aggressive

Passive

The Passives don't seem like threats because they sit quietly, not bothering anyone and not participating in office activities. They seem helpless, powerless, and inhibited. They prefer to follow the lead of others and they fear taking initiative. They rarely express feelings and have little self-confidence. They put themselves down. Their lament is "Why do bad things always happen to me?" They are the "poor me" types who never contribute and who drain the energy from any group. They seem unable to make choices and want you to make those for them. They avoid problems. They don't contribute and often impede the process.

Here are three types of Passive personalities:

▶ The empty seat

▶ Never on time

▶ The nice person who can't get anything right

The Empty Seat

Riktors comes to the meetings but never offers any suggestions or help. He sits in the cube next to yours and doesn't participate in any team projects, doesn't interact with co-workers, doesn't invite any office camaraderie. He doesn't share information or respond to inquiries about his work. While his work is okay, it could be more effective if he asked for or encouraged input from others. He just isn't there.

Never on Time with Anything

Well-intentioned, agreeable Joanna always offers to do things for everyone. She'll write your proposal, be on the committee, and pick up your laundry. But because she offers so much to so many, she can't get it all done. Adding to her dilemma, she's so eager to please that she spends more time on the unimportant than on getting the real job done. She didn't have the reports you asked for two weeks ago because she sent them out for special binding so they would look nice. She suffers from wanting to be helpful and you suffer because she's not getting her work done on time.

Nice Person Who Can't Get Anything Right

She is the twin sister to Never on Time. Every time Delores brings in a report there is an error, often a major one that has to be corrected before the report can be submitted.

She's always so apologetic and offers to correct it immediately but there will undoubtedly be another error in the next version. She's kind and she works well with everyone but during crunch time or at the end of the month, no one wants her to help. It will take more time to fix her mistakes than it is worth.

Indirect

The Passive-Aggressive (Indirect) personality types are one of the most difficult to confront. They can seem supportive and compliant but after you walk away from the conversation they will turn on you. They use manipulation, revenge, and trickery to get what they want. You never really know what they are thinking or feeling. They're hard to pin down on any agreement and you can never be certain that what was said between you will stay there. They smile at you while spreading stories about you to others. They may outwardly accept the problem, but keep the anger inside so it can last a long time. Another reason Passive-Aggressives are difficult is that they come in many forms and aren't always clear about their motives.

There are many distinct types of indirect personalities:

▶ All talk and no results

▶ Mr./Ms. Negative

▶ Devil's advocate

▶ Been there, done that

▶ The gossip-monger

▶ The sniper

▶ The know-it-all

All Talk and No Results

This is the Harry Potter character, Professor Lockhart, who talks about his many adventures, his accomplishments, and his amazing feats of daring—none of which have been observed by anyone but are all gloriously recorded in his many autobiographies. In your office, he might say, "At my last job, where I was in charge of the whole IT project, we were successful in making extraordinary changes in record time. I don't understand why you have such a problem here." But he never seems able to correct the problem or succeed in carrying out his own projects.

Mr./Ms. Negative

This type has something negative to say about everyone and every idea. They call themselves the realists and often see themselves as offering the other side of an idea or proposal. "The new website has a nice look to it but I don't think it's worth the money at this time." "Once again I'm afraid that Janice has taken on too big a project for her skills and abilities." These statements may seem thought-provoking. But when these difficult people always see the negative side of every idea, proposal, and change, they become less thoughtful and more provoking. They use up time making complaints and causing unnecessary work.

Devil's Advocate

The Devil's Advocates take pride in their ability to ask the "hard questions" about everything—usually very late in the process.

Anna is making the final presentation on a new tech project that has been in the works for six months. She feels she's done her due diligence, has been inclusive, has studied the opportunities and dangers inherent in this organizational change, and she's ready to get the go-ahead from the executive team. She's even taken time each week to update the senior executives individually. Now she's just giving them the timeline for the final steps. Anna sees that the COO, Eileen, has a list of questions as she always does. In their last meeting Eileen seemed very pleased with the plan and promised her support. Now, however, Eileen wants to know:

1. Why do we need to move ahead so quickly?

2. Does it make sense to hand this next step over to another project manager?

3. Does Anna think the team is really knowledgeable enough to move this forward or should they look for outside help?

Anna feels blindsided. She thought she had done everything to prepare for this meeting but Eileen wants to be thought of as thorough and tough.

Been There, Done That

This can be a boss, a peer, or someone who definitely feels she should not be reporting to *you*. They let you know that every idea you have has been thought of before, thoroughly vetted, and determined to be useless.

"We tried something just like that 5 years ago. We couldn't make it work then and I know we can't make it work now." The variables in those statements are time and people. In an organization's history, 5 years ago is a long time and just because it didn't work then doesn't mean, in this economy, with this technology, and this new breed of customers, that it won't be amazingly successful. And the people issue isn't the same either. Maybe they weren't trained well or prepared for the change. Of course, there is always the possibility that the former project didn't succeed due to lack of good leadership.

There are two variations of this type:

► **"This is the way we all have to do it."** There is a template that must be followed by each and every one. There is *one* process, *one* system, *one* procedure. No one can deviate from the path that has been so carefully defined for years, even though the path doesn't seem to be going in the right direction anymore.

► **"My Way"** is the theme song for Bob. He's going to do it the way he has devised for himself, even though his methods won't sync up with the rest of the team. "I've been doing it this way for years. It works and I don't see any reason to change."

The Gossip Monger

The Monger spends time gathering personal information and sharing it with as many others as possible. He often will offer this in a friendly, caring manner.

Jason just wanted others to be aware that, "I saw Diane and Dave together at the local pub after work. It's nice that they can relax like that together before going home to their families."

There is also the gossip who goes a step further and embellishes the story, but again couches their tale in a language that seems compassionate and certainly not a story that originated with them. "I just heard from someone in Finance that Bert is getting moved to another floor. That seems to be a demotion but I'm not sure how that will be seen by people in his department." Innuendo is their special talent. They also consider themselves great networkers. They want to be everyone's go-to best friend. They can engage anyone in conversation. But beware—whatever is revealed to them immediately enters the public domain.

The Sniper

These are like the Gossip Mongers in that they aren't having the conversation with you but about you with someone else. However, they often have a more malicious plan in mind when they share their information about others.

You've finished the meeting and it went better than expected. You got through the agenda, everyone agreed on major issues, work assignments were handed out, and the meeting ended a few minutes early. You stepped into the copy room to pick up some materials for the next meeting and you heard Bill sharing his version of the meeting with your boss and it doesn't sound like the same meeting. "We didn't get done what I'd hoped today. We talked a lot, but there were no real solutions and we wound up with more to do. We just finished up early without any real direction."

You think back to his participation in the meeting and wonder how he could so misrepresent what was going on. In the meeting he offered information, seemed very involved in the discussion, and took on some responsibilities for moving forward. Where did all of that go and what do you say to him and to your boss?

Snipers are a problem you usually don't expect and while they may not be difficult to your face, they cause a lot of trouble of which you are unaware. They can do all of this with a façade of good intentions. Bill's followup comment to the boss was, "I think Elizabeth means well, but she just can't handle projects this large. She'll need a lot of help and I'll certainly do what I can." The message is clear that you are not the person for the job. Because the message is stated in such a helpful manner, it's even more damaging when you try to defend against it.

The Know-It-All

They are the true experts. They are productive, energetic, and creative. They are difficult because of their attitude of superiority. No one else's ideas have merit. No one else's experience is worth anything. They take the air out of room and everyone just shuts down.

Aggressive

The Aggressive personality is the one most feared. These difficult people are expressive to the extent that they humiliate and devalue others. They are vicious and egocentric. It's all about them. They devastate others. This is the loud, yelling, arm-waving, finger pointing co-worker whom no one wants to cross. He stands over your desk and gets into your personal space to intimidate you and you can't ignore him. He sees everyone else as someone to use. He will put you down as a way of making himself look better. The Aggressive attacks the person, not the problem.

There are several types of aggressive personalities:

▶ Loves the limelight

▶ The blaster

▶ The power-grabber

▶ The dangerous difficult person

Loves the Limelight

There are people who seem to enjoy being difficult. It's what gets them up in the morning, thinking, "Whose life can I make miserable today?" They cause everyone around them to be uncomfortable and sometimes, depending on their position, fearful.

The Blaster

These people are very public about their sniping. They let you know in front of the whole department that you are not qualified to be there, and that your work is substandard and waste of time. They don't seem worried about the effect on you at all. Then after a loud and horrifying display, they walk away and seem to forget it. Later, they will ask you for a favor as though nothing happened.

The Power Grabber

They don't include others in decision making. It's all about their own need for control. It was clear to everyone in the department that the new boss was different from the last one. Ralph had been there for 16 years, knew everybody's family, brought treats every Friday, and was generous with raises and special rewards. That was not Darwin's style. He called the first meeting 10 minutes after he arrived. He laid out objectives for the next three months without reviewing the work in process. He said he had been hired to shake things up and he wanted everyone to know he intended to keep his word. He ended the first staff meeting with the statement: "I start my day at 6:30 and those who hope to still be here in three months should do the same."

Over the next weeks Darwin handed out assignments, taking the high profile jobs for himself and loudly berating those whose work was not up to his expectations. His language was offensive. While he yelled directions at everyone, it wasn't clear that he had a real vision of the future. He never thanked anyone for their work. He said he didn't need to thank people for doing what they were paid to do.

The Dangerous Difficult Person

There are difficult people who are beyond the scope of this book. They may have mental health issues that keep them from being in touch with what is really going on. They may have serious value conflicts. They may be emotionally or physically abusive or their desire for power and control overrides their sense of right and wrong. They are intimidating, menacing, confusing, and scary. Sometimes they are terrifying to be around and it's likely that very little except professional interventions can change their behavior. They need to be handled by professionals.

"Anderson, everyone knows this is my private coffee stop."

Assertive

The antidote to the difficult personality types—the Passive, the Indirect, the Aggressive—is the Assertive person. This individual communicates directly. He or she is fair and honest, and honors agreements with others. The Assertive keeps composure, and attacks problems, not people, while being respectful, open, and confident. Organizations need more Assertive personality types.

Does this describe you?

Rewards for These Behaviors

There are rewards for all of these behaviors. The Aggressive most often gets what she wants because she comes across as self-assured, in control, and scary. The Indirect gets what he wants without having to confront the issues directly. The Passive gets to stay out of the fray so she is rewarded by not getting noticed. The Assertives are the ones who receive the real, long-term rewards. They get the best solutions, they maintain strong relationships, and they keep their self-respect.

TYPES OF DIFFICULT PEOPLE IN YOUR HISTORY

Take a minute and go back to your "History of Difficult People" and see if you can name the types of Difficult People who gave you the most trouble. (Aggressive, Indirect, Passive)

Age	Person	Personality Type
Preschool		
6–12		
13–18		
19–23		
24–30		
31–current		

Part Summary

In this part, we've identified the different types of difficult people you've dealt with through your life. More specifically, we've identified some useful characteristics and common "types" of difficult people. With this information, you are better able to recognize these people behaviorally, and to determine what they are seeking through the behavior that is causing you difficulty.

How You

See and Hear

Difficult People

" *Arguing with a fool proves there are two.* "

–Doris M. Smith

In this part:

▶ How you contribute to the problem of handling difficult people and situations

▶ The role your beliefs play

▶ Using values to inform decisions

▶ A quick way to profile your own personality

How *I* Contribute to the Problem

Now that we've identified who *they* are and why *they* rate as difficult people, we need to reflect on what we bring to the mix. Each of us enters adulthood and the work world with unique life experiences and memories that set us up for dealing with difficult people in our own way. We received messages in childhood, either verbal or non-verbal, about how to treat people and be treated by others. From this we develop assumptions or beliefs about how the world *should* work. Along the way we develop preferences for how we like to learn, to live our lives, to make decisions, and to be with others. We also have values that are ours alone that guide our behaviors. Those values form the basis for our unique sense of purpose—our mission in life.

Every day we bring these personal rules and tools to our interactions with others—difficult or not. So before you begin to take on difficult people and *their* rules and tools, you need to look at what you bring to the equation. Messages, assumptions, beliefs, values, and preferences form our self-image.

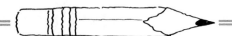

MESSAGES: *"MY MAMA ALWAYS SAID..."*

From the moment we are born, someone has been giving us messages about our behavior. Check the messages you heard in your childhood and add any other messages you may have heard that impact your behavior today.

❑ You need to be nice to everyone no matter who they are.

❑ You need to stick with your own kind.

❑ We don't fight in our family.

❑ We always fight for what's right. We stand up for ourselves.

❑ The teacher/coach/minister is an adult and adults are always right.

❑ Don't talk back to your elders (bosses, anyone in charge).

❑ It's most important to be the best at whatever you do—work, school, sports, and friendships.

❑ It's important to always tell the truth even if it might be hurtful to someone.

❑ It's important to be liked by everyone.

❑ We don't want to cause anyone harm.

❑ You need to do something right, or don't do it at all.

❑ If you can't say something nice, don't say anything at all.

❑ You go back there and punch him in the nose.

❑ If you don't whip him, I'll whip you.

❑ Don't get dirty.

❑ If you ignore them, they'll leave you alone.

❑ _____

❑ _____

Beliefs

The messages we received in childhood about how the world works stay with us into our adult years even if we don't remember the exact words. We turn those random messages into beliefs that guide our behavior in all areas of our life.

A child who came home from school with A-minus papers and whose Mother said, "An A-minus, why not an A?" may have heard:

"You need to be perfect."

Or

"You'll never be good enough."

Or

"You can do even better."

If you think you can, you can. And if you think you can't, you're right."

–Mary Kay Ash

"I hope my little outburst yesterday didn't upset you, Shipley."

BELIEFS

Fill in the responses you might have for these incidents:

1. Your very difficult boss calls you into her office to complain about an error in the financial report you just submitted. Because you have always believed, "I can always do better," what might be your response?

   _____

   _____

   _____

2. You're giving a presentation to a large group of your peers. Your assistant, who has been very busy, prepared the slides. In the middle of the speech you realize an essential slide is missing. If you feel the need to be perfect, what might be your response?

   _____

   _____

   _____

3. Your customer calls for the second time today to ask if someone else can come take a look at the sprinkler system your company just installed. You believe that you'll never be good enough. What is your likely response?

   _____

   _____

   _____

IDENTIFYING YOUR BELIEFS

Which of these do you hold to be true? Check the box beside those you relate to.

- ❏ I have to be liked.
- ❏ I always have to prove myself.
- ❏ I am here to serve others.
- ❏ I am basically defective.
- ❏ I must not forgive myself if I have fallen short of any goal or personal standard.
- ❏ The world owes me a good life.
- ❏ Life is fair.
- ❏ Life is unpredictable and scary.
- ❏ I have to win.
- ❏ I have to find a solution.
- ❏ I can't be wrong—it's somebody else's fault.
- ❏ I can't lose.
- ❏ I have to be perfect to be accepted by others.
- ❏ People who care about each other should never fight.
- ❏ I have to please everybody.
- ❏ There is enough joy for everyone.
- ❏ I have to try to see through someone else's eyes.
- ❏ Other people should meet my expectations.

Values

What are three words, chosen from among many, that clearly articulate what you believe to be your guide in life?

▶ What are those words that define what you stand for?

▶ What words are clear in all your actions?

▶ What words have others heard you use to evaluate a difficult situation?

▶ What words do you live by?

You choose. You articulate it. You act on it. You are known for it. Having a strongly held value that is in conflict with another person's strongly held value can escalate a discussion to the level of dealing with difficult people. Clarifying your values gives you a very quick check on your level of frustration with a customer or co-worker and it can help you to understand the range of values that can be important to others.

"Sorry, Bill, I know that it's important for you to have a top (quality) product here. But I need to cover my costs on this project and I just don't see how I can give you that carpet upgrade when it wasn't included in the estimate."

While we can't ask all our customers and co-workers to submit their list of values, we can identify our own. Look at the list in the next exercise and choose three or four words that describe what you hold to be most important in life. Do you value achievement over all? Or is beauty something without which you could not live? Do you crave a challenge in all you do or is it more important to be competent in all you do?

It's not hard to make decisions when you know what your values are."

–Roy Disney, American Film Writer and Producer

VALUES CLARIFICATION

Choose three or four words or phrases that guide your personal and professional life:

Achievement	Flexibility	Power
Advancement	Forgiveness	Productivity
Adventure	Freedom	Profitability
Artistic Expression	Friendship	Quality
Beauty	Fun	Quantity
Belonging	Generosity	Rationality
Caring	Growth	Recognition
Caution	Health	Relationships
Challenge	Helping	Respect
Communication	Honesty and integrity	Responsibility
Community	Human relationships	Risk
Compassion	Independence	Security
Competence	Individualism	Self-acceptance
Competition	Influence	Self-control
Consensus	Inner harmony	Service to others
Contribution	Innovation	Speed
Control	Involvement	Spiritual growth
Cooperation	Knowledge	Stability
Courage	Learning	Task focus
Creativity	Loyalty	Teamwork
Curiosity	Nature	Tolerance
Customer focus	Order	Tradition
Determination	Organization	Uniqueness
Diversity	Perseverance	Variety
Economic security	Personal growth	Wealth
Fairness	Play	Wisdom
Family contentment	Pleasure	

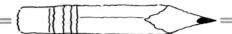

VALUES INTO DECISIONS

Eliza has just come into your office demanding that she be given the job title that Matt has. They have been with the organization the same amount of time but their work assignments have been very different. Matt has clearly taken on more responsibility and he has been a dynamic team player.

Eliza lets you know that it is very important to her that she be treated fairly, that she is be given an opportunity to grow in this company, and she wants people to know that she has a lot to offer.

1. Identify the values that are being articulated.

   _____

   _____

   _____

2. What are the discussion points you may want to explore regarding the values you may share?

   _____

   _____

   _____

3. Where might there be an opportunity for resolution?

   _____

   _____

   _____

Notes:

   _____

   _____

   _____

   _____

   _____

Preferences/World View

At the end of a very busy, exhausting day which would you rather do?

▶ Go out with a group of friends for dinner and some dancing.

▶ Go home and curl up with a good book.

Using that simple inventory can help groups or individuals see that the person who seems to be very difficult is really just someone who sees the issue from a very different perspective.

Several behavioral researchers have developed personal preference inventories. These include the Myers-Briggs Type Indicator and the Keirsey Temperament Sorter.[1] To get a brief overview of how these inventories can help you begin to identify those differences, answer the following questions:

QUICK PERSONALITY PROFILE

For each question, circle the letter of the response that best describes you.

1. If after a hard day at the office, the way you get energized is:

    E. Go out to dinner and comedy club with your team (**Extrovert**).

    I. Go home and read a book all alone (**Introvert**).

2. If you are more comfortable with:

    S. Facts and details (**Sensing**).

    N. Visions and grand plans (**Intuition**).

3. If you make decisions based more on:

    T. Logic and rational thinking (**Thinking**).

    F. Emotional response and feelings (**Feeling**).

4. If you would rather:

    J. Make and follow your plans (**Judging**).

    P. Take a chance on plans evolving (**Perceiving**).

Put the 4 letters you circled together to form your profile: ___ ___ ___ ___

---

[1] For more information on the Myers-Briggs Type Indicator, visit www.mbticomplete.com. For information on Keirsey, visit www.keirsey.com.

Now imagine that you identified your preferences as INFP—an introvert, who is visionary, makes emotional decisions, and makes plans with an eye to what might change. Your customer just came in eager to have lunch with you again today. Her lunches often last one to two hours. She wants to discuss the details of her latest project and has a lot of questions. You've already provided answers but will need to repeat them. She wants an immediate response to cost overruns she described earlier this morning, as well as a completion date.

You may be guessing that she's more E – extroverted, S – more detailed, T – thinking, and certainly more J – get the job done now. That would probably make her your exact opposite. But being alert to her preferences can help you give her what she needs or help you explain in her language why that can't happen just the way she demanded.

In this case, the best working relationship with your extra-extroverted customer may be that you agree to a working lunch but let her know that your time is limited—so you can get back to work on her deadlines and extra orders.

Difficult people may be those who simply see the world differently than you do. If you have taken a personality assessment such as Myers-Briggs, you know there are certain things about the world that are clear to you but don't even register with others. Once when I was doing a preference assessment with a group of physicians, one very young doctor came up after doing the assessment and made this statement: "I don't see how anyone could have answered those questions any differently than I did." That sounds like the height of arrogance but there are many of us who have wondered the same thing.

This is how I learn, work, make decisions, and plan my day. I think any other way would be so _____ (fill in the blank).

If you make decisions easily based on just the facts and logic (Thinking), imagine how difficult it would be to work with someone who always has to base every decision on how it would affect the feelings of others (Feelings). If you really dislike making changes when you have perfected a routine that works (Sensing), imagine sharing an office with someone who is always trying a new approach (Intuition). At the end of the day you are exhausted by the arguments that ensue.

When working on a project with someone, your approach is to keep focused, decide quickly, and stay with the plan (Judging). Meanwhile, your partner wants to remain open and flexible and include as much information as possible before setting down the plan (Perceiving).

There are people who need to start their day at the office by greeting everyone, checking on the families, pets, and holiday plans before they can get to work (Extroverts). They always seem to sit next to the person who arrives early and is well into their very quiet, intense work, and who does not need to know everything about his co-workers (Introverts). Which one of these is most like you? And which one is most like the last difficult person you dealt with? Sometimes this is simply a failure to communicate, because both parties believe their focus is universal.

We can't change the messages we heard in childhood. And some would say we can't change our personality profile. But we can be aware of the messages and our way of seeing the world. Our approach to conflict is learned behavior. That means that whatever we have learned, if it isn't working for us, can be unlearned. New methods can replace old ones. If you remember that your approach to each difficult person is a learned behavior, then you can step back and examine your behavior and the learned behavior of the difficult person as a starting point for resolution.

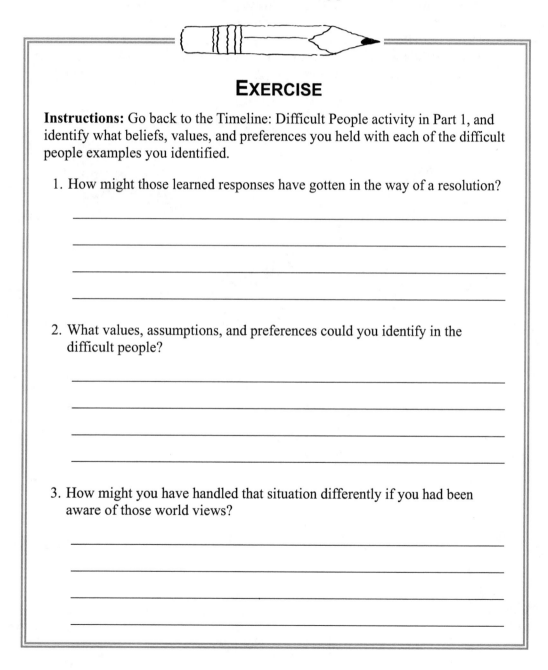

EXERCISE

Instructions: Go back to the Timeline: Difficult People activity in Part 1, and identify what beliefs, values, and preferences you held with each of the difficult people examples you identified.

1. How might those learned responses have gotten in the way of a resolution?

_____

_____

_____

_____

2. What values, assumptions, and preferences could you identify in the difficult people?

_____

_____

_____

_____

3. How might you have handled that situation differently if you had been aware of those world views?

_____

_____

_____

_____

Part Summary

In this part, we discussed the importance of understanding several of the ways you shape your approaches to dealing with difficult people based on who you are: your personal belief system, your personal values, and your preferences, how you energize yourself, how you prefer to make decisions, and how you like to operate with respect to your decision processes. This important information allows you to bring more depth to your understanding of the conflicts and difficulties you face. You can use this information to avoid difficulties in some cases, and to gain a clearer understanding of how to directly pursue your needs in other situations. You've also had a chance to apply some of this awareness to some "live" situations you have faced or may be facing presently.

The Power of a
Difficult Person

"The result of long-term relationships is better and better quality, and lower and lower costs."

–W. Edwards Deming

In this part:

▶ You'll learn more about the impact difficult people have on you.

▶ You'll examine the degree of difficulty they produce.

▶ You'll discover the power and impact of role relationships.

Degrees of Difficulty

Some of you might consider the outbursts of a co-worker to be bearable. Some of you might think you can deal with the loud and aggressive types as long as they know what they're doing. But some of you might be at the point where the person in the next cube who hums all day long has finally inspired you to find a job in another department, at another company, or on another planet.

What's your threshold of pain when dealing with difficult people? What can you ignore and what drives you to think dark and dangerous thoughts? You can place each of the types of difficult people into one of these categories. Your ability to handle each type or your tolerance for some behaviors is determined by how much discomfort they cause you.

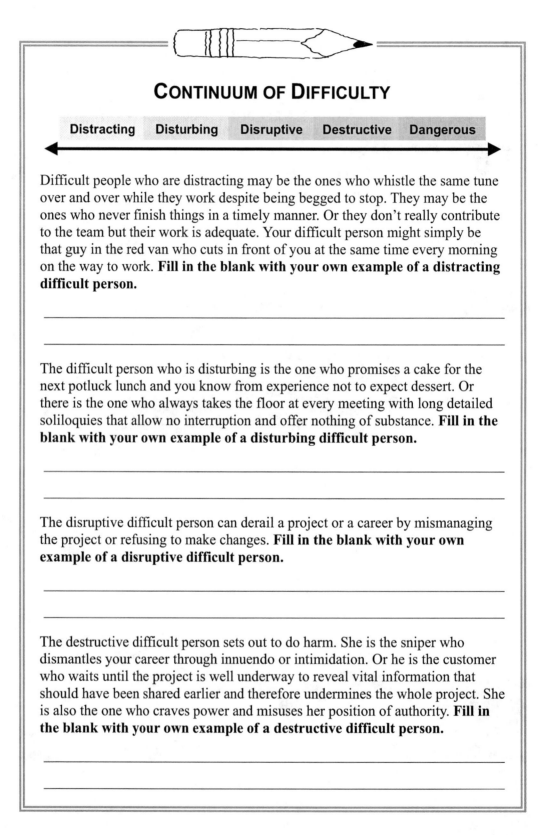

CONTINUUM OF DIFFICULTY

| Distracting | Disturbing | Disruptive | Destructive | Dangerous |

Difficult people who are distracting may be the ones who whistle the same tune over and over while they work despite being begged to stop. They may be the ones who never finish things in a timely manner. Or they don't really contribute to the team but their work is adequate. Your difficult person might simply be that guy in the red van who cuts in front of you at the same time every morning on the way to work. **Fill in the blank with your own example of a distracting difficult person.**

_____

_____

The difficult person who is disturbing is the one who promises a cake for the next potluck lunch and you know from experience not to expect dessert. Or there is the one who always takes the floor at every meeting with long detailed soliloquies that allow no interruption and offer nothing of substance. **Fill in the blank with your own example of a disturbing difficult person.**

_____

_____

The disruptive difficult person can derail a project or a career by mismanaging the project or refusing to make changes. **Fill in the blank with your own example of a disruptive difficult person.**

_____

_____

The destructive difficult person sets out to do harm. She is the sniper who dismantles your career through innuendo or intimidation. Or he is the customer who waits until the project is well underway to reveal vital information that should have been shared earlier and therefore undermines the whole project. She is also the one who craves power and misuses her position of authority. **Fill in the blank with your own example of a destructive difficult person.**

_____

_____

Placement on the Continuum

That driver in the red van may move up from distracting to dangerous if he does this every day and is clear that it is about challenging you. And the gossip monger could simply be distracting because nobody ever believes what he says anyway. By assigning your difficult person to a place on the continuum, you can begin to see the power they have over your life and determine what measures to take to change the balance of power.

Role Relationship

There is another element in the assessment of difficult people to consider—pecking order. Is the difficult person the "Boss of me"? Or are you the Boss? That may make a big difference in how you present a problem to your boss about his inability to ever run a meaningful, worthwhile meeting. Or are you the customer who thinks he is always right because it says so right there on the slogan on the wall?

A co-worker may someday be the "Boss of all" because she's clearly on her way past all of the others on the team. So how can we find the most effective ways to deal with her sniping behaviors now in a way that can create the best boss of tomorrow for everyone?

Power

There are several attributes besides titled position in a company that can confer power on people and give them a sense of authority. Helplessness, surprisingly, can be one of those, as in, "Oh, poor me. I need your help so desperately. I can't succeed without your invaluable help." This can be followed by long sigh and sad smile.

Connection to Power

If your boss is powerful and you are her trusted, valued employee, then you have referred power. "My boss says to tell you that we can't have reports of this quality being handed in. You'll have to redo them and get them back to me by Thursday at the latest."

Titles and Places

If you have a real office instead of a cube, then you must be very important to the company and I will need to take you very seriously. If you also happen to be seen in the company of the Senior Vice President of Marketing at a lunch, that's even more power to you.

Knowledge

People who know other people, know the industry, and have book smarts or education carry the power of their knowledge. There is value in being able to pick up a phone and find answers for others—to have at hand information critical to a project.

Self-assurance

Some people have a strong, positive, internal sense of self. It may come from having attachment to power, titles and places, and knowledge; but it also comes from a deep self-knowledge and self-acceptance. These are the people with whom you are comfortable because they seem comfortable with themselves. They can laugh at their own mistakes. They are eager to learn new things. They aren't threatened by others' need for titles, places, authority, or knowledge. And they are rarely on anyone's list of difficult people.

All of these—customers, bosses, direct reports, peers, and team members—can be difficult people at work and you need to make some adjustments in your strategies for each category.

A DIFFICULT PERSON IN YOUR LIFE

Describe one type of difficult person who is currently complicating your life.

_____

_____

What is the profile of this difficult person?

_____

_____

_____

Do you see them as Aggressive, Indirect, or Passive?

_____

What level of difficulty are they causing you?

_____

What is your relationship to this difficult person and what special circumstances need to be considered when dealing with him or her?

_____

_____

_____

_____

What gives them their power over you?

_____

_____

_____

_____

Favorite Difficult Person

One of the reasons the TV show *The Office* is so popular is that many of us can relate to at least some of the characters. Some are exaggerated to provide comedy, but some seem too real and too personal. We find ourselves saying, "That's the guy in my office."

And we have all had our "favorite" difficult person, the one we hate to be around but love to tell others about.

"Can you believe my boss/co-worker/mother-in-law, customer from...?"

"Let me tell you what s/he did yesterday!"

Some difficult people do bring us a measure of satisfaction—if only after the fact.

THE DIFFICULT PERSON YOU LOVE TO HATE

What is your favorite difficult person story?

_____

_____

_____

Who is the difficult person you love to hate?

_____

_____

_____

_____

First Response

CASE STUDY: First Response

You are 20 minutes late for the baseball game—again—and stuck in traffic. There is a woman two cars ahead of you who is tying up traffic for at least a mile. She seems to be looking for something in the back seat and is oblivious to the long line of angry, honking drivers behind her. You honk too, thinking more noise is better.

Why does this always happen to me? How inconsiderate of her. Looks like she's looking for her phone. I get so frustrate with people like this who just seem so out of touch.

Maybe she doesn't care about her kids—but I do and I need to get to that game on time today. He'll be so sad if I am late again. Last week I missed his one and only hit and he was so disappointed. This just infuriates me! Come on, lady, get on the road.

You honk your horn. You feel your heart speed up and you're feeling very warm.

You pound on the steering wheel and throw a fit in the privacy of your own space.

Just then you see the ambulance come up behind you and you are close enough to see the attendant rush to the back seat of the car, grab a tiny child and begin what looks like resuscitation. The mother is standing there helpless, crying and suddenly all your initial reactions—your *first response*—seem so completely unacceptable.

You think of your own child and remember a similar time. You feel an immense sense of guilt for the feelings you had two minutes ago. You hope that there will be a successful ending to this drama.

All of this within 3 minutes!

WHAT DO YOU SEE?

Which of the following math problems do you notice first?

A.	$10 - 5 = 5$	C.	$25 - 5 = 20$
B.	$16 - 8 = 4$	D.	$17 - 7 = 10$

If you noticed question B first, that's because we are drawn to notice what is wrong or bad. We need to keep that in mind with our first responses. We want to be aware of what is wrong, but react in an appropriate way.

Most of us would like to think of ourselves as being mature adults who can properly manage our emotions. When faced with another incident involving a difficult person, however, our first response is often less mature and more visceral than we'd like to admit. We get a negative adrenaline rush and we go into a "Rapid Response Mode." We have stomach-clenching, teeth-grinding reactions. Our heart rate speeds up. Our palms get sweaty. We sit up straighter or we slouch back and hide. We react. And it seems almost impossible sometimes to hold those reactions inside long enough to get the whole picture.

"Mr. Bennett has abruptly left the company."

FIRST RESPONSE

You look up from your desk and see your sales manager walking—make that *storming*—toward you with that look of fury in his eyes (again.) The last time he had that look he chewed you out for giving a customer a 5% discount on merchandise damaged during delivery.

What is your *first response*? Check those that you think would be your response.

❑ **Fear** – He is going to fire me, yell at me, humiliate me, or dock my pay.

❑ **Frustration** – Here he comes again to waste my time with some petty issue.

❑ **Guilt** – What have I done now? It must be really bad if he's so angry.

❑ **Indignation** – Who does he think he is charging up to my desk with that attitude? He's not so great.

❑ **Pushed into a corner** – He is coming right for me. I have no escape

❑ **Always/Never** – He never asks me what I think could have happened.

❑ **Blame** – This is all about his problems.

But what if what's really happening is that the sales manager isn't upset with you at all? He just lost a big sale and he is heading for his office. Your desk is just on the way there. All that energy was expended for nothing.

Do-Overs!

How many times have you walked away from a situation thankful that you didn't act on your first response? We need to acknowledge those first responses and then recall the times when our first reactions were not helpful.

DO-OVERS

Recall a time when you had a very strong reaction to a difficult person.

1. What were your first responses?

   ❑ Anger?

   ❑ Attacking?

   ❑ Other

2. What was the actual situation? Briefly describe it here.

   _____

   _____

   _____

3. Reflect on what you now know to be true about that situation. What was different about the situation (than you initially thought, and) that you didn't learn until after your initial responses?

   _____

   _____

   _____

4. How might the situation have been improved by weighing all the factors *before* you reacted?

   _____

   _____

   _____

5. What can you learn about handling difficult situations from this brief activity?

   _____

   _____

   _____

FIRST RESPONSE

Consider the last difficult person incident you experienced.

1. What emotions did you experience as a result of your first response?

_____

_____

2. What actions did you take?

_____

_____

_____

3. What do you know now about that situation or persons that you didn't at first?

_____

_____

_____

4. What would you do differently if you were granted a do-over?

_____

_____

_____

Getting Past the First Response

Emotions are indicators. They can warn us about impending danger. They can give us clues about our world before we are even mentally attuned. But they can also deter us from working through an issue with a difficult person because we go forward without all the necessary input.

The third time the customer at the health club walked in to complain, Elsa heaved a great and very audible sigh. She stood up and put her hands firmly on the counter and leaned forward. She asked in her most dismissive voice, "What now, Jane?" And that felt so good for about 15 seconds until Jane put her hands on the counter, leaned right back at her and let her know that there was a lot more to talk about regarding the trial membership plan she signed up for. The customer isn't always right. Jane has had many complaints about many small issues.

Elsa secretly hoped that Jane would drop out after the trial membership and not sign up for a full year package. There was just one problem with that, though. Even though she complained constantly, Jane had brought five friends to the club, all of whom had purchased memberships. If Jane stays on as a client, she will probably continue to bring Elsa more new business.

GETTING PAST THE FIRST RESPONSE

What could your response be to the situation described between Elsa and Jane?

_____

_____

_____

_____

_____

_____

_____

_____

Go, No Go

Assess the situation. All of us have these difficult people in our lives. They exist. Everyone knows them. You know your tolerance for the difficulty with which they plague you. Now you have a choice to make:

Do you really want to deal with this difficult person?

You can decide the situation is too risky and learn to live with it. You can decide that the situation has to change for the good of the organization. Or you might decide that the only option is to leave the organization. Is it worth your time and energy to deal with this difficult person? There may be rewards but there are also potential hazards.

The next exercise provides a fairly long list of questions to consider before you decide how to move forward with the difficult person. There's an excellent chance that some of these are in the back of your mind already. It's better to consider them in advance than to have to deal with them on the fly.

When you reach the end of your rope, tie a knot in it and hang on."

–Thomas Jefferson

RISK ASSESSMENT

Use the following list to assess whether or not you want to deal with this person.

1. Who is the difficult person?

2. What is their type?

3. Are they passive, aggressive, indirect, or assertive?

4. What level of discomfort does this person pose for you?

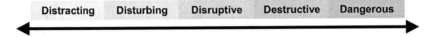

| Distracting | Disturbing | Disruptive | Destructive | Dangerous |

5. What is their role with respect to your role (boss, co-worker, customer, direct report, team member)?

6. What are their attributes of power that may have an impact on the outcome?

7. Do those attributes matter to you?

8. What is the tolerance of the organization for dealing with difficult people and conflict?

9. What are the messages from the organization about how to deal with each of these types of people?

10. Do you deal differently with your customers than with co-workers?

11. What have you seen others do when dealing with difficult people that was or was not effective?

12. What are the costs of confronting or not confronting this individual?

13. Are there any of your beliefs or values that are being called into question that make this essential to address (beliefs and/or values)?

14. What personal preferences are affected by this dilemma (energy, learning, decision-making, planning)?

15. Is this your issue to solve, or someone else's?

16. What fears do you think this difficulty between you might reveal?

17. Identify the impact you think this difficult person's behavior is having on the team/group/organization/you/others.

CONTINUED

18. Is there potential for positive resolution or not?

19. If it can't be resolved, is there someone who will need to be told?

20. What do you perceive to be your way of handling conflict?

21. Are there alternatives? What are they?

22. What is the payoff if you handle it differently?

23. What are the potential consequences of leaving things as they are?

24. Does this challenge your integrity or the integrity of the organization?

25. Is it likely to change without a confrontation?

26. If it doesn't get better, is it likely to continue to be a problem or get even worse?

27. If it does continue, is it likely to have a negative impact on your future?

Decision Time: Go or No Go

Which path do you decide to take?

- ❑ The risk is too great to address this difficulty—I will live with it.

- ❑ There isn't enough difficulty to fuss about—I will learn to cope.

- ❑ I'm better off leaving—this is an intolerable situation.

- ❑ I need to wait for a better time.

- ❑ Maybe this will resolve itself.

- ❑ Go.

If you have decided that this situation with your particular difficult person needs to be resolved, then it's a GO.

Part Summary

In this part we've discussed the tendencies many of us bring to our "immediate response" when we confront a difficult person in our lives. Often the result of our learned behaviors growing up, these patterns become habitual and show up as immediate emotional reactions to the threat we perceive when confronting a difficult person. We discussed strategies for choosing different and, hopefully, more productive approaches to dealing with these situations. We also presented a risk assessment tool to give you some help in assessing the situation to determine if a direct confrontation is the best strategy, or if another approach will be more productive for you. This process of considering the situation without being "driven" towards a predictable, habitual response gives you more opportunity to manage yourself appropriately and to make a considered decision about your next steps.

Making a Plan and Finding the Words

> *Remember not only to say the right thing in the right place, but far more difficult still, to leave unsaid the wrong thing at the tempting moment."*
>
> —Benjamin Franklin

In this part:

▶ How to plan to deal with a difficult person

▶ Strategies for dealing with Indirect, Passive, and Aggressive types

Planning to Deal with Difficult People

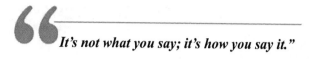

It's not what you say; it's how you say it."

That's the old axiom, but it's only partly true. Your facial expressions, body language, the questions you ask, and your perceived position of power in a confrontation all matter a lot. But choosing the right words is the place to start.

Because your approach to dealing with difficult people is a learned behavior, you can unlearn it and learn new behaviors that serve you better. You already identified the idiosyncrasies of your current difficult people and you learned that you bring your own set of tools and rules to the exchange. Now take time to examine some of the factors that can improve your interaction. Begin by finding a quiet place to be alone with your thoughts. Take a deep breath and consider the essential elements for dealing with difficult people.

PLANNING FOR DIALOGUE

1. Describe the specific precipitating incident. In other words, "What happened?

   a. What did the difficult person say or do that signaled a warning?

      _____

      _____

   b. What were the circumstances that just preceded it?

      _____

      _____

   c. Who was there? What was said?

      _____

      _____

   d. What was it so significant about this incident?

      _____

      _____

2. Describe the problem.

   a. How did that incident contribute to a larger struggle with this individual?

      _____

      _____

   b. How has this now become a pattern of difficulty between you?

      _____

      _____

   c. What one sentence would best explain the nature of this problem?

      _____

      _____

CONTINUED

Handling Difficult People and Situations

3. Describe your reactions.

   a. How are your beliefs, values, and feelings affected by this problem?

   _____

   _____

   b. What about your personality was being called into question?

   _____

   _____

   c. What were you feeling?

   _____

   _____

   d. What were you thinking about?

   _____

   _____

4. Describe your preferred outcome.

   a. What positive outcome can you imagine?

   _____

   _____

   b. What would you like to have happen?

   _____

   _____

Strategies for Dealing with Different Types

Now, we'll talk about strategies for dealing with types of difficult people:

▶ Indirect

▶ Aggressive

▶ Passive

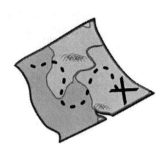

Dealing with the Indirect Types

At last week's all-hands meeting, Bill took the opportunity to once again *publically challenge a decision of yours* in front of all 55 attendees. He asked the questions in an information-seeking manner but it seemed clear to you that his intent was less about the information and more about making you uncomfortable.

Here are some questions you might consider:

1. Describe the specifics of the precipitating incident.

    a. What did he ask?

    b. What was happening with the others in the meeting?

    c. What was your response?

    d. What was the outcome of the conversation?

    e. What else happened in the meeting?

2. Describe the problem.

    a. Was this a single incident or is this a pattern with Bill?

    b. What is the core of this concern for him?

    c. What is the whole picture?

    d. How does this single incident encapsulate a larger problem you have with Bill?

    e. What is that larger problem?

    f. How would you state the difficulty you often have with Bill around this issue?

3. Describe your reactions.

    a. What feelings were evoked by this incident and by his pattern of similar behavior?

    b. What did you think he was trying to do at the meeting?

    c. What are some of your concerns about other times he has shown this same behavior?

4. Describe your preferred outcome.

    a. How do you want to be treated by him?

    b. How can you meet his needs for information?

    c. Are there other issues that compound this one?

Strategies for Dealing with Indirect Types

A sniper, for example, won't confront you directly. It will require extra effort on your part to draw out this person's true responses. The sniper is likely to dismiss the issue and to deny that a problem exists. He wants it to be all about you and your misunderstanding. A sniper's primary strategy is to keep you "off the scent" by shooting at you and keeping the focus off of his real issue. He will take shots at your role, your contributions, your thoughts and ideas, and any other areas he can find to criticize or comment on. The most difficult thing about him though is that all of these things happen behind your back. When he's in the room with you, everything is "fine."

"I was too busy shopping in Paris to read your notes."

Dealing with the Aggressive Types

Nelson scares everybody. He walks into the office and people seem to disappear. Today's tirade has to do with overtime costs. He throws the timecards on your desk, demands answers to why, who, and how, then walks out with just a backward comment such as, "Get that information to me in an hour." Unfortunately, he holds the key to that information because he has been the one authorizing the extra time. Now that his boss is upset, he needs to find a scapegoat and you're it today. Last week it was Tim and the week before it was Angie. It seems to be your turn.

With the Aggressive type, consider these questions:

1. Describe the incident.

    a. What did he ask for?

    b. What was your response?

    c. What was the outcome?

2. Describe the problem.

    a. What else was happening around this issue?

    b. Was this a single incident or is this part of the pattern?

    c. What is the core of this concern with him?

    d. What is the whole picture?

    e. How does this single incident encapsulate a larger problem?

    f. How would you state the larger problem?

    g. How would you state the difficulty or issue?

3. Describe your reactions.

    a. What feelings were evoked by this incident and by his pattern of similar behavior?

    b. What are some of your concerns about other times he has shown this same behavior?

4. Describe your preferred outcome.

    a. How do you want to be treated by him?

    b. How can you meet his needs for information?

    c. Are there other issues that compound this one?

Strategies for Dealing with Aggressive Types

Aggressors want to dominate any discussion and keep you from expressing yourself. They are willing to raise their voice and push for an action "right now!" You need to present a confident, forceful case. And you need to manage your feelings so you don't become intimidated by their manner. Sometimes the Aggressive types will push hard just to see if they can "win" by the force of their approach. If you don't appear intimidated, you can "change the game" to one that is more reasonable and considered.

Dealing with the Passive Types

CASE STUDY: Apologetic Annabelle

Annabelle has just brought in the receipts for the week and there is a $7,000.00 error on one of the invoices she already sent out to the customer. She's apologetic, smiles, and says she's sure she can fix it. But the last time that happened, the customer refused to pay and said he'd pay exactly what the invoice said, and we could live with it or he'd take it to court.

Annabelle is a Passive type. Here is a framework for dealing with such a person.

1. Describe the incident.
2. Describe the problem.
3. Describe your responses.
4. Describe your desired outcome.

Strategies for Dealing with Passive Types

They won't want to interact at all. They will smile and go away. You need to find the words to keep them focused. Ask specific questions to elicit the most open feedback.

Part Summary

In this part, you received a template to guide you in choosing the "right words" to deal with your difficult situation. You learned how to describe the event that precipitated the difficult situation, to describe the problem, describe your response, and describe your desired outcome. You also received guidance on how to apply this template with difficult people who are Indirect, Aggressive, and Passive types. Finally, you applied the template to a practice exercise related to your own difficult person.

Leading a Difficult Customer to a Better Outcome

"*Have a heart that never hardens, a temper that never tires, a touch that never hurts.*"

–Charles Dickens

In this part:

▶ The LEAD model for dealing with difficult people

▶ How Appreciative Inquiry might lead to a world without difficult people

The LEAD Model

You have probably been involved in a conversation where you thought, "If only she hadn't yelled at me, I could have given her exactly what she wanted." If your face says one thing and your words another, it's very difficult for people to react exactly as they should. Once you have decided on the words, it is just as important to consider how to deliver them and how to react to the responses you may get.

LEAD stands for Listen, Explore, Attend, and Deliver the solution. This is an easy way to remember the importance of *how* to approach every difficult exchange. Your manner and approach, and the way you present your words, can make all the difference in a successful outcome.

LEAD is a strategy to help you maintain your composure and work through a difficult situation with appropriate openness—enough to maintain a non-defensive posture so that you can identify the real problem. You address the problem "on point" and in a way that satisfies you and your customer—the difficult person on the other side of the situation. Here is a brief overview of the steps:

Listen. Our first tendency when we're having a difficult conversation is to get defensive and make sure we don't lose. Therefore, the emphasis is on *speaking* to what we think and believe is the right outcome. The problem is that we frequently try to fix the problem with solutions that don't work because we've short-circuited our opportunity to hear and understand what happened. We confuse understanding with agreement. And we don't want the other party to think we agree with him or her. Listening to understand is the first step in successfully dealing with difficult people.

Explore. With good questioning techniques, we create the opportunity to fully understand what happened and how the difficult person experienced it. The reasons for the feelings become clearer and those feelings become less intense as the difficult person gets a chance to express them in an open manner. You also demonstrate your willingness to be influenced by the difficult person as you ask and listen for understanding.

Attend. Using your whole being, stay focused on *the other party* and on *his or her problem* until it is fully expressed and he or she feels understood. Attending includes your body language, your eye contact, and many other behaviors.

Deliver. After you listen, ask questions to fully understand, and attend to them, you are positioned to respond with your thoughts about how to address the situation. It will be on point and will address their issues more fully because you have taken the time to listen to them and to understand where they are coming from.

Listen

How good are you at listening—really listening? "Yah, uh huh, I hear ya. Sounds fine to me."

Imagine for a moment that for your customer, Rachel, you are the difficult person and she has decided to let you know about it. She walks in the office, stands with her hands on her hips, and says:

"Yesterday, I asked you to be at my house at 3:30." (**Description of the Incident**)

"You never show up when you say you will." (**Description of the Problem**)

"I am angry and frustrated about not getting this unit installed before the other workers are scheduled." (**Description of Responses**)

"I need to get this project done and I need you to take it seriously. I want to know what you are going to do about it." (**Description of Desired Solution**)

She has managed to thoroughly *describe* the situation and you have certainly gotten the message but she may get more results if she takes time to *listen*.

At the local appliance store, Jim and his mother were attempting to buy a new computer for her. She was very frustrated by all the choices she had to make. Buying the last one was so much easier. Jim wants to buy one in her price range and get out of the store. "Just find us a basic model and we'll figure it out later" he tells Roger, the sales clerk who is trying to help.

Here's a process to follow:

1. Listen.

2. Show respect and regard.

3. Make eye contact.

4. Use positive verbal cues.

5. Use supportive non-verbal cues.

6. Paraphrase the concern.

7. Encourage freedom of expression.

Listen Because You Want to Understand

How important is it that you hear their side of the story? You will have to care about the other person and be willing to accept that he or she may have great insights and a better solution than you do.

For Mom, this is a large investment and a huge learning curve. For Roger, it means a satisfied customer who believes the store motto that the customer is always right. Jim's side of the story is that he has been through this before and really does know what his mother needs.

Show Respect and Regard for the Other Person

Is one of your beliefs that everyone has a right to be heard, to have an opinion, to see the world differently than you do? Then your words and body language will indicate that you give weight and value to what you are hearing. You are willing to take the time to admire the difference of opinion.

Make Eye Contact

While it is very important to have clear, open-eyed contact with the other person, there are extremes here too.

Too much intensity—staring your difficult person down will change the balance of power and can derail the dialogue. You can look at them, blink, and look down at your notes. Really seeing someone and noting their facial expressions and body language is as important as hearing the words.

Use Positive Verbal Cues

These are the constructive words you use to encourage more discussion.

"I think I can understand what you mean. I can certainly see what that could be like for you. Tell me more about that. How would that look to you?"

"Yes."

"I see."

"Okay."

"Certainly."

"Good."

What are the short phrases that will bring forth more pertinent information?

Use Supportive Non-verbal Cues

There are the occasional very loud messages you give off by just nodding, smiling, covering your mouth with your hand, or folding your arms over your chest. What is your body saying?

Welcoming Cues	Non-welcoming Cues
Smiling	Frowning
Nodding	Shaking your head
Leaning forward	Leaning way forward or way back
Arms or hands opened	Covering your mouth

Paraphrase the Concern

Another method for bringing clarity to a situation is to repeat what you heard with slightly different words, and in an understanding or sympathetic tone.

Encourage Freedom of Expression

It takes a bit of courage to elicit a response that may be in direct conflict with how you see things. Do you really want to know that someone is hurt, angry, or saddened by something you may have done? Without that knowledge you may have to travel this path of conflict again.

"I need you to be completely honest about the way you saw this event today so we can make sure it doesn't happen again. I want to know what part I may have played in that incident so I can improve my performance around that next time."

Review of Rights

Everyone has rights and having this list handy will keep you and the difficult person stay on track.

Everyone has the right:

- ▶ To make good choices for themselves
- ▶ To be treated with respect
- ▶ To have and express their own feelings and opinions
- ▶ To be listened to and taken seriously
- ▶ To set their own priorities
- ▶ To say no without feeling guilty
- ▶ To ask for what you need.
- ▶ To get what you pay for
- ▶ To make mistakes
- ▶ Not to assert themselves
- ▶ To change their minds
- ▶ To disagree
- ▶ To have their needs be as important as those of others
- ▶ Not to like everyone
- ▶ To see the world in their own way

Explore

Explore the other person's point of view. Any solution will be minimized without that input. This task requires you to suspend judgment and action while you search for all the relevant facts and feelings around this issue. It requires the skillful use of questions to help the customer fully share the situation as he or she experiences it. Done properly, you help the customer unload his or her feelings and view of how it all came about. In the process, you all calm down, and both you and the customer gain a clearer understanding of exactly what happened.

CASE STUDY: The Furious Trimmer

Alan was furious. He wanted his yard to look perfect for his daughter's high school graduation party, but his brand new weed trimmer wasn't doing its job. As he looked around the yard that night during the party, he could see the ragged untrimmed patches, and he got mad all over again.

The next day he was back at the store still fuming about the yard's flawed appearance during his daughter's big celebration. The clerk saw him coming and as soon as she heard what happened, she gave him a new weed trimmer and sent him on his way.

This sounds like the right approach, except that Alan will tell this story a hundred times and be mad every time. He will not be a repeat customer. How different it would have been if the sales clerk had taken the time to Explore. "Tell me what happened? Sounds like that was very disappointing to you on that special night. I wish we could have helped you out with that yesterday. Let me see how we can make this…"

While asking the questions to better understand, there are some other guidelines to help you shape your behavior in a constructive, results-producing manner:

- ▶ Maintain your composure.
- ▶ Stay engaged.
- ▶ Maintain a professional approach.
- ▶ Pay attention to the body's physical needs.
- ▶ Use open-ended questions.
- ▶ Use directives to gain more information.

Maintain Your Composure

It is very tempting to confront the difficult person with the fullness of your frustration. You may really, really want to yell over the cube to the person who has been whistling their own little tune, over and over (and also very badly) for the last 2 hours while you are trying to finish a detail report. Or, imagine how satisfying it would be to tell the customer that you don't believe for a minute that there was a problem with the weed trimmer yesterday. That you know he just wants to return it! Although it may be gratifying for the moment, in the long run it could be destructive to relationships and, even worse, you may now be seen as the difficult person!

Unfortunately, when we are dealing with difficult people we may also have let the situation go too long so when we finally decide to get it resolved, we feel a great sense of urgency. That just heightens our apprehension. In both cases, we need to focus on being calm.

Stay Engaged

Although there are short-cuts to solutions, often they turn out to be much less satisfactory than staying with the issue until all the concerns have been aired. Keep asking the questions until you are certain there is nothing more that will come back later as a problem.

Maintain a Professional Approach

► **Dress**: In some companies there has been a change in dress code that encourages more comfort and informality our business attire.

While you don't want to come into a very casual office setting with black suit and tie for your meeting with your difficult person, you may need to give some thought to what you can wear that will eliminate self-consciousness. This is a meeting about an important subject and important people. You don't want to find yourself wondering if your blue striped tie matches your suit.

► **Touch**: Maintaining professionalism also means considering the impact of physical contact. Shaking hands, putting your hand on someone's shoulder, and patting their hand are all part of the professional concerns that are intensified in difficult situations.

▶ **Distance**: You may need to think about where you need to sit or stand for the most impact or the least intimidation. Sitting directly across the table from someone may seem too direct. Sitting beside them may not give you the opportunity for eye contact that you need. If the table is too large or too small, that may add a complication for someone who is already wishing to avoid this conversation. If the room is very small, it can feel claustrophobic but a very large room for just two people can also add a negative feature. Find a space that feels comfortable for you and then offer several options for seating.

Pay Attention to the Body's Physical Needs

It might seem like preparing to deal with a difficult person is like training for the triathlon. Do you really need to be mentally alert and in top physical condition to take on the mighty challenges of Sue, the Office Dragon? Not necessarily. But there are things you can do to prepare for the offensive that may be coming your way.

▶ **Get some exercise**: Take a walk, preferably out of the building, to clear your head and get fresh air and oxygen into your brain. Go for a swim. Jog around the block.

▶ **Get something to eat:** A good protein snack will give you energy and calm you. Get real food. Skip the sugar, which will work fast but then take you into a dive.

▶ **Get something to drink:** Water preferably. Drink something that can keep you from having a dry mouth and difficulty thinking and speaking clearly.

▶ **Get a good night's rest:** You want your mind at its best. Just before the meetings, try to find some time away from the noise and chaos for a short time will help you to gather your thoughts.

Use Open-Ended Questions

Asking the open-ended question is a way of gaining more information. Use the following as a guide to give you a much fuller picture of the situation.

Describe the Incident:

▶ How did you see that incident yesterday?

▶ What did I miss? Where was the customer when all that was happening?

Describe the Problem:

▶ Does this seem like a part of a larger issue?

▶ What have we done with this in the past?

▶ What is your concern with this incident?

Describe the Responses:

▶ What were you thinking about when that happened?

▶ Did you have any strong feelings about that?

▶ What did you assume I would do?

Describe Desired Outcome:

▶ What do you need from me to make this work better?

▶ How can you help me with this?

▶ What are some of the possible solutions we would both agree to?

OPEN-ENDED QUESTIONS

What are some of the other open-ended questions Roger can ask Mom and her son to do a better job of finding her the right computer, and possibly even meet the son's needs to get a quick decision? Write four questions here that you think would help Roger get to the bottom of this customer's difficult decision?

1. _____

   _____

2. _____

   _____

3. _____

   _____

4. _____

   _____

Use Directives to Gain More Information

Sometimes people just need a little nudge to get them to open up about more information that would expand the possibilities for closure. Directives are simply statements about what would help you to better understand. They guide the customer to talk about the areas that will add the most value to your understanding.

▶ Tell me a bit more about the connection you see between this problem and...

▶ Say some more about how you see that working.

▶ Fill me in more on that option.

Use Closed-Ended Question to Get Closure

If you want to get a computer that is in your price range, has the three features that you like on your old one and I can find that one in stock for you, would the two of you be very happy to get out of here and get back home to set it up today?

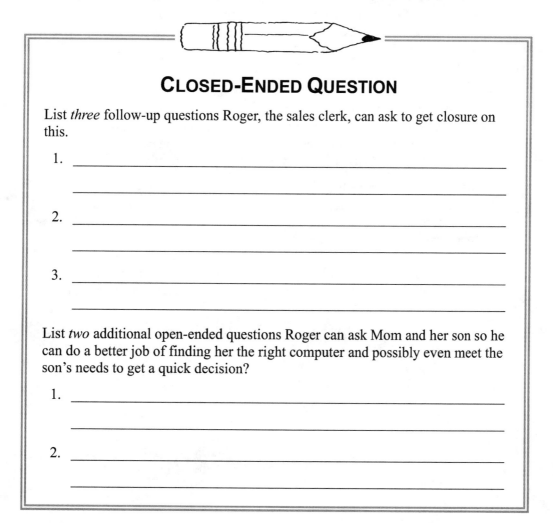

CLOSED-ENDED QUESTION

List *three* follow-up questions Roger, the sales clerk, can ask to get closure on this.

1. _____

_____

2. _____

_____

3. _____

_____

List *two* additional open-ended questions Roger can ask Mom and her son so he can do a better job of finding her the right computer and possibly even meet the son's needs to get a quick decision?

1. _____

_____

2. _____

_____

Here are a few more guidelines:

▶ **Be Authentic**: Using "I" statements to let others have clear insight is another critical feature when dealing with difficult people. If they don't know who they are dealing with, they can't open up and be genuine in their reactions or their input. I believe, I sense, I saw, I want, I will do, I suspect, I observed, I noticed, it is my opinion.

▶ **Be Transparent**: Use words whose meaning is clear. How can you make your meaning visible to the other person in a manner that will elicit that same transparency in their words? You have to be able to be open and let it show. It isn't enough to say what you think they want to hear.

▶ **Offer Self-disclosure**: You've just spent several pages describing your assumptions, values, and preferences, so you are prepared to take that remarkable, unique, and perhaps a little bit unusual self into the discussion with the difficult person. Knowing yourself is just a part of the job. Accepting yourself is the next step that leads to self-confidence. "I know who I am and I believe I am worthy of seeing the world differently, expressing my thoughts and opinions, and being listened to." Just keep in mind that the difficult people are bringing their own unique composition too.

▶ **Be Congruent**: The words you say have to match the language of your body. Smiling while you tell someone how angry you are that she's always late can destroy the whole effect. Keeping a serious but still open look on your face while delivering very harsh criticism isn't an easy task but it sets the tone for the discussion and sends a clear message of your intent.

▶ **Be Explicit**: After planning, preparing, and worrying for 5 weeks, you finally decide to approach the subject of Emily's repeated tardiness. You do a masterful job of describing the precipitating incident that brought you into this meeting. You talked all about your response to it and then you left her with a lot of questions about what exactly you wanted her to do about the whole thing. Or, you told her what you wanted her to do but neglected to share any of the specifics about where this came from and why you are calling it to her attention now.

Be specific about what happened, what you believe to be the problem, your responses, and your intentions for resolution.

Attend

You need to be alert to the difficult person's reactions to the discussion.

CASE STUDY: It's All about Shelly

Shelly has been doing most of the talking to Alex about his frustration with the direction they've chosen. She sees it as her problem and is determined to be a gracious co-worker. Five minutes into the conversation she notices that his arms are crossed tightly in front of his chest, and he has turned away from her to gaze out the window. She does a quick check of herself and realizes she has clenched fists, a loud voice, and she's leaning across the table and into his space. Attention. Attention. Attention.

Why do you suppose Alex looks ready to bolt out of the room? Be able to pick up those clues before they get too far. Watch for averted eyes, tension in hands, direction of body, tempo of the words, and volume and pitch of voice.

The attentive listener should:

▶ Pay attention to the other's demeanor.

▶ Ask further clarifying questions.

▶ Track.

▶ Encourage good timing and pacing.

Pay Attention to the Other's Demeanor

Good listening engages your whole body. Leaning forward is not necessarily the preferred stance. It can be intimidating. Setting way back in your chair may make you seem distant. A better approach is mirroring.

Mirroring means meeting the other person's spatial needs. If they move forward for more direct conversation, you can move slightly forward into the discussion. When they pull back to get some space, move back and give them that space. Nodding in response to their nod suggests that you are following their thoughts.

"Bill, it looks like you are moving closer and closer to that door so I think that probably means I need to step back from this a little. We looked at the facts but I know there must be a solution you'd be happier with. What are your suggestions?"

Ask Clarifying Questions

"I guess you'll have to explain that procedure you use again. I don't quite understand all the aspects of it."

Track

It is often difficult to focus on what the difficult person is saying, feelings, and doing and at the same time consider what your response needs to be. Are you asking the right questions? Are you using the right body language? Did you wear the right shoes today? Will I finish this in time to get to the train? Will I have a job tomorrow if I don't fix this in the next 10 minutes?

Encourage Good Timing and Pacing

Knowing the right time to talk about something and when to take a break from the conversation so you can both step away and get some perspective is an essential ingredient in this. When you can see and hear that you're not agreeing on the best next step, it is sometimes helpful to be able to say "We have really had a good discussion, but my head is so full of thoughts and ideas that I need some time to clear my head and think about all of this. Let's get back together in an hour and see how we are feeling about a resolution."

Deliver a Solution

It is so tempting to give someone a solution (*the* answer, my best advice, the right understanding of the policy, and so on). "Here, just take the day off and go." "Great, you can have it your way on this." It seems to save time and a lot of energy to just jump to the conclusion and get someone out of your office or out of your face. However, delivering a real solution, while it takes a little more effort, has far more potential for building relationships. Here's the process:

1. Summarize your understanding of the concern.

2. Specifically respond.

3. Gain commitment or a next step.

Summarize Your Understanding of the Concern

So many small words and gestures have undoubtedly added up to result in this level of difficulty. It seems almost impossible in highly charged situations to be an excellent listener, explore all the facets of the discussion, AND attend to the fine nuances of people's body language and facial expression. To ensure that you have not missed some essential element, now is the time to summarize what has been said.

You want to give each person another opportunity to get past the unpleasant incident that initiated this dialogue.

▶ Describe the problem in your own words.

▶ Ask for confirmation of that description.

▶ Describe your responses to the problem, your beliefs, and your feelings.

▶ Ask for confirmation of responses.

▶ Describe your wishes for resolution.

▶ Ask for suggestions for resolution.

CASE STUDY: The Truant Worker

Stephanie, your direct report, took a vacation day without asking.

Describe the Incident

"Stephanie, you took a vacation day yesterday without checking to see who else was on that shift and what the workload was going to be. We've talked about your vacation leave plans several times over the last few weeks."

Describe the Problem

"Let me see if I have all the correct information about how this occurred because we have to guarantee total coverage and we need to be able to count on you."

Describe the Response

"I was very concerned that you didn't talk to me before you left for the day."

"What did you think would be the outcome?"

Specifically Respond

I have listened to your description of what happened and have gathered all of the information I need to fully understand. I have checked my understanding by summarizing and sharing my understanding of the situation as you see it. You have confirmed that my understanding is complete and correct. Then, I can respond to the situation. My response should be "on track" with your experience of the problem. The response is "surgical," meaning it is precise. It is not "off track" and irrelevant to your needs or your view. "Based on your description of what happened this time, I recommend that you…to avoid a similar problem in the future."

Gain Commitment, or a Next Step

I appreciate your candor. I think we can arrange to have that kind of a communication system set up to cover us when we are overwhelmed with customer calls. I'd like you to let the others know that this is how it will work and I think it is best if we get the word out today and the system in place by Thursday. Are you willing and able to get that done by 2:30p.m.?"

CASE STUDY: The Blaster

Bill is a Blaster who charged into your team meeting and loudly expressed his frustration with you and your whole team for not getting the reports he requested for his California regional director. He spent 5 minutes telling you how useless your department is to his directors, how you never get the right stuff done on time, and so on, and then he walks out.

You calmed your team and let them know you'd get back to them the next day with the outcome of your conversation with Bill and you continued with the meeting.

You catch Bill in the hallway an hour later and when he sees you coming he smiles and asks how your weekend was. When you ask to talk about what he said in your meeting, his reply is, "I just needed to blow off some steam. We did get those reports. They were a little late but I just forgot to check." Then he starts to walk away. You ask to talk to him in half an hour and you go back to your office to think about that conversation.

Listen: What specific Listening skills will be most important here?

_____

_____

Explore: What specific Exploration skills will you use?

_____

_____

Attend: What Attending skills will be helpful in this situation?

_____

_____

Deliver: How would you summarize and close?

_____

_____

Being the Difficult Person

Your attitudes and behaviors are always on display to internal and external customers. Unfortunately a bad, grumpy morning may be remembered for months by a large number of non-returning customers who didn't know what was behind that mean-spirited look. They won't know you'd just hung up the phone after a conversation with your remodeling person and learned that the cost of the job had doubled. The first customer in line saw the face meant for the remodeler but it was memorable enough for them choose another café next time.

When do *you* get to be the difficult person? How about when a customer is yelling at you in front of everyone and using words that aren't appropriate and loudly maintaining that it is all your fault? You'd really, really like to respond in kind with the same tone and volume and some words of your own and you're pretty sure you know whose fault it is!

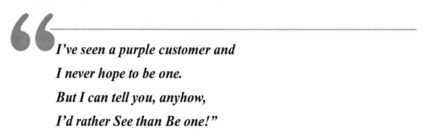

I've seen a purple customer and

I never hope to be one.

But I can tell you, anyhow,

I'd rather See than Be one!"

–Freely adapted from "The Purple Cow"

When a difficult customer comes up to you ready to take you on over poor service, bad products, or broken promises, you don't have to give them exactly what they're demanding. Nor do you have to stand there and be publicly humiliated or threatened. You do need to use all your very best LEAD skills to find a resolution and maintain the customer relationship.

Begin with respect and regard because as hard as it may be in the moment, everyone, even purple customers, deserve that. Make eye contact and maintain your composure. This is about trying to find a solution together, so you will need to Explore.

Handling Yourself

What questions will you need to ask to sort out a problem when you would really like to be the difficult person?

▶ "I can see how frustrated you are. Let's try to figure this out. Start from the beginning, and tell me what happened…"

▶ "Tell me more about that."

▶ "Then what did you do?"

Attend to them by offering to move to a quiet place to talk more. Then try to find a solution together.

Your role is to provide a calming environment, listen attentively, ask for more information, be present in the conversation, suggest solutions, and in the midst of all that, set limits and be assertive. The customer has rights but so do you.

The outcome you want isn't friendship but a customer who feels heard and can go away from the conversation with their self-esteem intact and with some likelihood of retuning as a good customer.

You are the manager of your internal difficult person. There are times when what you would most like to do is out of the question. Take a deep breath and remember to Listen, Explore, Attend, and Deliver.

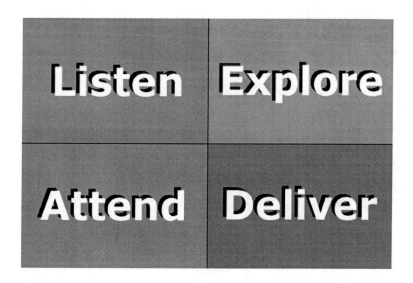

Appreciative Inquiry

It would be a wonderful world if everyone got along and enjoyed and celebrated their differences. While this might be fantasy in the broader world, it's possible in the smaller scale; that is, it's in your power to create an organization in which people interact optimally. In 1990, David Cooperrider of Case Western University created a model for organizations that describes a process that promotes positive growth and change. He called it *Appreciative Inquiry*—it's an approach to organizational change that concludes that if you take the time to ask questions in a thoughtful and positive manner, you are much more likely to get a collaborative response.

Appreciative Inquiry focuses on the strengths and successes of co-workers, a group, a team, a unit, or a whole organization, and then finds ways to build on those strengths for even greater success.

The process of identifying what has been done well energizes groups. It gives people a sense of pride in their labors and an opportunity to be positive, even in difficult situations.

Unfortunately, strategies for organizational change often focus on deficits. For example:

▶ Where did we go wrong?   ▶ Where were our mistakes?

▶ What isn't working?   ▶ Whose fault is this?

This negative focus leads to:

▶ Blaming   ▶ Power grabbing

▶ Excuses   ▶ Manipulation

▶ Defensiveness   ▶ Incompetence

▶ Resistance   ▶ Low morale

▶ Fatigue

Not surprisingly, these things create a negative culture, a breeding ground for unproductive behaviors. The following table describes some alternatives using the Appreciative Approach.

Problem Solving Approach	The Appreciative Approach
Focus on deficits	Focus on what works
Identification of problem	Valuing the best of "what is"
Analysis of causes	Envisioning what might be
Analysis of possible solutions	Dialoguing about what should be
Action planning	Innovating – what will be
Basic Assumption:	**Basic Assumption:**
Organizations are problems to be solved	Organizations are centers of infinite human capacity

When the Appreciative model is introduced it's sometimes doubted because the language of the initial questions seems too soft or nice. For example:

► What works here?

► What do we do better than anyone else in the industry?

► What have been our major successes?

► When did you feel most engaged with and excited about a project?

► When have you worked with a dynamic team?

► What made these experiences so unique and memorable for you?

► What were the elements of your successes?

These are questions that uncover the richness of organizational experience. Once people begin to share these experiences, they tend to think of more, and then they add to those until the energy in the group shifts. Team members begin to smile more, to laugh about the things that didn't go so well.

The group moves from skepticism to possibilities. They are filled with optimism and anticipation. When the group focuses on the causes for their success, they can begin to find ways to replicate them and discover pathways to even more successful projects. Even more important is that they know what success looks and feels like, and they know they can do it again. In environments like this it's hard for a difficult person of any kind to get a hold on the group.

In short, the Appreciative approach:

▶ Describes what is working well and celebrates successes.

▶ Describes the strengths of the group.

▶ Identifies the possibilities for building on those strengths and past successes.

An example of the Appreciative approach might be to ask the following questions:

▶ Evelyn, you've worked in this division for 4 years and I'm curious what is it about this job that brought you to us?

▶ Evelyn, what did you hope this job would be?

▶ What is it about this job that you enjoy most?"

Inquire Appreciatively

Ask positive questions about the work they do, the people with whom they work, and what intrigued them about the job when they started. For example:

▶ What would make this work even more enjoyable and meaningful for you?

▶ How can we make that happen?

▶ How can I help you to get some of the less satisfying work completed so you can get on to what you enjoy most?

Your inquiry should feel non-threatening, curious, and sincere. It may be that the individual has untapped talents. While the assignments still need to be done in a timely manner; the individual is more likely to respond to your requests if he or she feels valued and believes that there will be more interesting work to do in the future. This approach works with all types of people because it sets the tone and changes the culture to one that is positive.

Appreciative Inquiry: Summary

Appreciative Inquiry gives us options for resolving issues with the difficult person. Rather than attacking the person or backing away and not resolving the problem at all, we can look for what is positive in the situation and then find a common ground. The Appreciative approach takes some practice because we have learned to start such conversation by identifying the problem and the negative behavior. It takes a little more time to start with what is valued and what we are grateful for. Then the resolution comes more easily for both parties.

In a world that is exciting and growing and ever-changing, there needs to be people with unique and uncommon needs, wants, and ideas. Sometimes they can come across as difficult, or simply interesting, curious, and singular. We choose how we see them, how we work with them, what we learn from them, and how we are enriched by them. This requires us to slow down and LEAD—listen, explore, attend, and then deliver a solution or give back to others in full measure.

Part Summary

In this part, we've discussed how to deal with a difficult person who is your customer. In some instances, your options are more limited in terms of how you deal with the difficult person you are confronted with. In some cases, your primary role is to work with customers who bring their difficult problems to you because you are paid to be in that role. In those instances, it is entirely inappropriate for you to demand or expect that your customer should refrain from sharing their upset with you. Your job is specifically designed to fulfill that role for your organization. In those instances, you need to encourage customers to share those problems and concerns, and your job, generally speaking, is to find solutions to their problems. In this last section you have been given a process model to guide you in working through those problems to help your customers arrive at a solution to their problems that is on track and appropriate to meet the promise that your company or organization has expressed or implied through the sale of your products. LEAD is a tool to help you maintain a customer-focused, solution-seeking set of behaviors that creates loyal customers.

A P P E N D I X

Additional Reading

Block, P. *The Empowered Manager: Positive Political Skills at Work.* San Francisco: Jossey-Bass, 1987.

Bradberry, T., & Greaves, J. *The Emotional Intelligence Quick Book: Everything You Need to Know to Put Your EQ to Work.* Fireside, 2005.

Brinkman, R., & Kirschner, R. *Dealing With People You Can't Stand: How to Bring Out the Best in People at Their Worst.* McGraw-Hill, Inc., 1994.

Cava, R. *Dealing with Difficult People: How to Deal with Nasty Customers, Demanding Bosses, and Annoying Co-workers.* Key Porter Books, 1999.

Cooperrider, D., & Srivastva, S. *Appreciative Inquiry in Organizational Life.* In Srivastva, S., Cooperrider, D. L. (Eds.), *Appreciative Management and Leadership: The Power of Positive Thought and Action in Organizations.* Jossey-Bass Inc., 1990.

Keating, C. J. *Dealing with Difficult People: How You Can Come Out on Top in Personality Conflicts.* Paulist Press, 1984.

Nanus, B. *Visionary Leadership.* Jossey-Bass, 1992.

Pearman, R. R., & Albritton, S. C. *I'm Not Crazy, I'm Just Not You: Secrets to How We Can Be So Alike When We're So Different: The Real Meaning of the Sixteen Types.* Davis-Black, 1997.

Ratey, J. J., & Johnson, C. *Shadow Syndromes: Recognizing and Coping with the Hidden Psychological Disorders That Can Influence Your behavior and Silently Determine the Course of Your Life.* Pantheon Books, 1997.

50-Minute™ Series

If you enjoyed this book, we have great news for you.
There are more than 200 books available in the
Crisp Fifty-Minute™ Series.

Subject Areas Include:

Management and Leadership
Human Resources
Communication Skills
Personal Development
Sales and Marketing
Accounting and Finance
Coaching and Mentoring
Customer Service/Quality
Small Business and Entrepreneurship
Writing and Editing

For more information visit us online at

www.CrispSeries.com

HERE'S WHAT KIDS SAY ABOUT BOOKS IN THE
EARTH INSPECTORS™ SERIES!

"I felt like I was right there."　　—Derek Smith

"Very futuristic, exciting and even funny."
　　　　　　　　　　　　—Elizabeth Minet

"So good I didn't want to put it down."
　　　　　　　　　　　　—Amy Greene

"While you're having fun...you're learning also."
　　　　　　　　　　　　—Danielle Becker

"Exciting...full of surprises."　　—Tim Ferris

"I give it an A+."　　　　—Simon Smith

Books in the EARTH INSPECTORS ™ Series

EARTH INSPECTORS™

RUSSIA

What is the Golden Horde?

by Edward Packard

Illustrations by Barbara Carter

McGRAW-HILL PUBLISHING COMPANY

New York St. Louis San Francisco Auckland Bogotá Hamburg
London Madrid Mexico Milan Montreal New Delhi
Paris São Paulo Singapore Sydney Tokyo Toronto

EARTH INSPECTORS is a trademark of Metabooks, Inc.

Original conception by Edward Packard.

1 2 3 4 5 6 7 8 9   SEM   SEM   9 5 4 3 2 1 0

ISBN 0-07-048004-4

LIBRARY OF CONGRESS CATALOGING-IN-PUBLICATION DATA

Packard, Edward
  Russia: What is the Golden Horde? / by Edward Packard.
    p. cm.
— (Earth inspectors; 12)   Summary: As an Earth Inspector the reader is pursued by wolves in the Russia of Peter the Great, trapped with Czar Nicholas during the Revolution, and carried off to a gulag in Siberia.
  ISBN 0-07-048004-4
  1. Plot-your-own stories.   [1. Soviet Union—Fiction.
2. Time travel—Fiction. 3. Plot-your-own stories] I. Title.   II. Series
P27.P1245Ru   1989
[Fic]—dc19   89-12725
                                                    CIP
                                                    AC

Dear Reader,

Are there really aliens in outer space? Most scientists think it likely. And many people have tried to guess what they would be like.

If they were very intelligent and had invented spaceships, they might want to see what's happening here. After all, Earth is a *very* interesting planet.

Imagine how an alien would feel, after traveling trillions of miles in a spacecraft, to see a beautiful blue-white sphere growing larger and larger in the star-studded black sky.

Imagine *you* are that alien—one living on Turoc, a planet far more advanced than ours—that you are an Earth Inspector!

Edward Packard

"Here we go!" your friend Tang yells over the roar of the falls.

"Get farther back on your splash board!" you shout, but Tang is already over the rim, riding a torrent of water. You're right behind him, skimming on top of a great surging wave that's traveling on air!

"Woooooooaooooo!" You're soaring above the gorge, riding an arc of white water, then plunging, faster and faster, until, holding your splash board before you like the cutting edge of a knife, you dive into the deep, cool blue pool at the base of the falls.

You kick your way to the surface and paddle toward the riverbank. Tang is already standing there, shaking the water out of his soft white fur.

"That's ten runs for me," he says. "I'm hungry!"

"Me too," you say, and race him for the picnic pack.

While the two of you munch on berries and Nutra-Max bars, you ask Tang about his latest space voyage. Tang is a Vorkar Inspector and has made several trips to that planet.

"Is it true there's no nighttime on Vorkar?" you ask.

"That's true," says Tang. "There's also no daytime."

"Come on," you say, "there has to be one or the other."

"I'm not kidding," he says. "Vorkar doesn't have a particular sun. It's just floating alone in space, but it's in the Pleiades system, where there are lots of superbright stars close by. So, though it's always nighttime, it's also always daytime, because there are enough of these very bright stars in the sky to give light and heat."

"I'd like to visit there sometime," you say.

"And I'd like to visit the planet you've been inspecting," he says. "I've heard that Earth is fantastic."

An idea comes to you. "Tang—I'm going on an inspection trip to Earth in a couple of days. Let's ask Simbar if you can come along!"

Tang does a double backflip and lets out a whoop. "Great idea—let's do it!"

Go on to the next page.

You and Tang wait in the Chamber of Wisdom only a minute or two before you hear the sound of a pure harmonic chord. A graceful figure glides through the portal. It is Simbar, the Surveyor of the Spheres.

He has already received your thought waves and sent you his own. "Well, Tang," he now says aloud. "You've chosen a good time to apply to be an Earth Inspector—we need an extra person on the next mission to that planet."

Tang starts to do another of his backflips, but he quickly settles down as he receives Simbar's thought wave: *Please wait until after the meeting*.

Turning to you, Simbar says, "You better help Tang brush up on Earth facts. He should know, for instance, that gravity is a lot stronger on Earth than it is here on Turoc. Tang, you better not go riding over any fifty-foot-high waterfalls when you get there."

Tang nods his furry white head.

Simbar, receiving your thoughts, says, "So you're impatient to know about your mission. Well, I won't keep you waiting. I want you and Tang to land in the biggest country on Earth. It's called the Union of Soviet Socialist Republics."

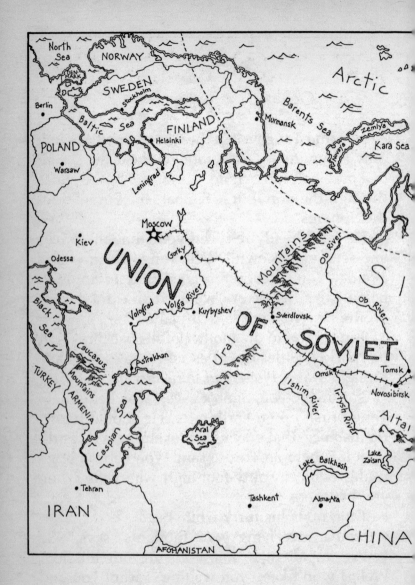

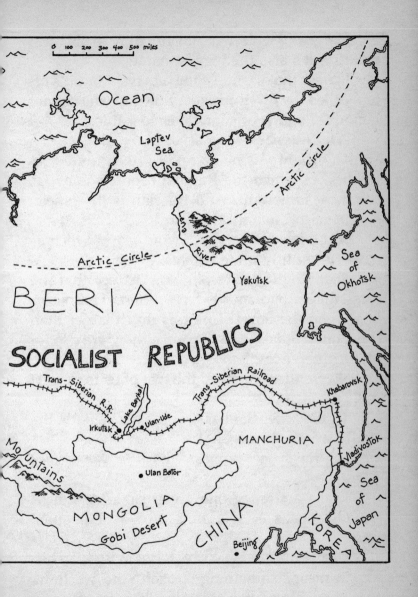

"My gosh," you say. "It's not only the biggest country, it's also the biggest name!"

"I guess that's true," Simbar says. "But it's often called by its initials—USSR—or the Soviet Union for short, or sometimes just Russia."

"Why Russia?" Tang asks.

"The country is made up of fifteen united republics, of which the Russian republic is by far the most important. And Russian is the official language throughout the country."

"Sort of like America," you say, "which is made up of fifty united states."

"That's right," says Simbar, "except that the Russian republics mostly have different ethnic origins, and the Soviet Union is much larger than the United States, and of course there are a lot of other differences."

"No wonder you need the two of us to inspect it," Tang says.

"By the way, Simbar," you say, "what's the riddle we are to solve?"

"It's this," he replies: *What is the Golden Horde?*

"That's a strange one," you say. "A 'horde' usually means a 'swarming crowd of people,' right?"

"That's true," Simbar says, "but in Russian history it means something special. And we think that the answer has a lot to do with the way Russians behave."

"And the way the Russians behave has something to do with the fate of the earth—right, Simbar?"

"Exactly. Now we have no time to waste. Prepare to leave at dawn tomorrow. Russia is a vast and sometimes confusing place. So be careful and use good sense. The power of Turoc be with you."

This said, Simbar stretches up to his full three-foot height. Like everyone on Turoc, he is almost oval in shape, with short little arms and legs, but his long, white fur is as fine as the down of a swan, and his green eyes as large as an owl's.

Simbar has barely glided out of the chamber when Tang does one of his double backflips.

"Hey, Tang," you say, "you better stop flipping and start checking out your Earth facts—we're leaving in just a few hours!"

Turn to page 8.

You and Tang complete your bioforming that night, each of you rearranging your molecules so as to form the shape of an Earthling—in fact, those a young Russian might have. At the same time you bioprogram yourselves to speak the Russian language, as well as other languages spoken in the Soviet Union.

You lift off at dawn, and within a few hours you're streaking past Turoc's sun, the great star Bellatrix. You're piloting your spacecraft, the *Voyager*. Tang's craft, the *Ranger*, is a few hundred yards off your starboard fin.

"Thirty seconds to the transit," you radio Tang as the *Voyager* passes Bellatrix's outermost planet.

"My co-coordinates match yours; all systems ready," he says.

"All right, let 'er go."

Tang's craft disappears into a halo of light.

"Ready, Chin Chin?" you ask your computron.

"Ready, Inspector."

"Very well then," you say. *"Transit!"*

Instantly the *Voyager* passes into the space–time continuum. In a wisp of time (for there is no other way of measuring it) your craft emerges near the moderately bright yellow star that Earth-lings call the sun. Though you've traveled an enormous distance from Turoc—470 light years—you're still in the same corner of the Milky Way galaxy, which itself is 100,000 light years across!

Now, deep within the solar system, the *Voyager* streaks toward its destination at a few million miles an hour. Soon you're so close to Earth that it takes up almost a third of the sky. The portion beneath you is all in the northern hemisphere. A white glare shines off the planet's polar cap, a ragged-edged disk of ice and snow more than a thousand miles across. Swirling white clouds block parts of the surface, but you can make out the outline of all of Asia and eastern Europe. Most of the northern tier of this vast expanse is made up of a single country—Russia.

Turn to page 91.

Moscow's subway is surprisingly clean and efficient, and cheerfully lit by crystal chandeliers. There's no trash lying around or graffiti on the cars. No wonder the people of Moscow are proud of it. You ride to the end of the line and then walk to the entrance of the highway heading east. After a long wait, you're able to get a ride from a friendly truck driver bound for Omsk in western Siberia, only a few hundred miles from Novosibirsk. Ivan, the driver, tells you he's never heard of the Golden Horde. He seems nervous about having offered you a ride—perhaps he's afraid he'll get into trouble. In any event, he has little to say, and so, for the long trip, there's nothing for you to do but look out the window at forests and fields, factories and farms, mile after mile after mile. At night Ivan sleeps in the cab, while you sleep in the back of the truck shivering under a moth-eaten bearskin rug.

There's finally relief from the monotonous landscape when you reach the Ural Mountains, 1100 miles east of Moscow. The road winds through passes between snowy, forested slopes. The sun shines brightly, and daylight lasts until

12

well into the evening. The spring thaw has arrived, and rivulets from melting snow trickle across the road.

You pass a boundary stone that marks the division between Europe and Asia, and soon afterward, another one that says, *"Entering Siberia."* Then the land flattens out again. For the next two days, you continue on across grassy plains spotted with clumps of birch and aspen.

Early one morning you reach Omsk. Ivan lets you out on the highway outside the city.

Turn to page 72.

A few hundred miles above the earth's surface, you bid Tang good-bye and order Chin Chin to set the *Voyager* on course for the eastern end of the Soviet Union.

You're preparing for landing and have descended to about twenty miles above Earth's surface when a warning light flashes on.

"Chin Chin, what's happening?"

"Soviet radar picked us up. I had to engage our stealth gear to throw them off. They have very strong air defenses around Vladivostok."

"I thought that—"

Chin Chin interrupts: *"Missiles converging. Hit probability ninety-three-point-five percent."*

"Time evasion," you shout. Your words are almost drowned out by a high-pitched whine as the *Voyager* performs an emergency maneuver. Then all is calm again, and your spacecraft is steady on course as if nothing had happened.

You glance at the instruments. "Chin Chin, did you send out a signal to the *Ranger*?"

"It was sent out automatically," your computron replies. "But we've no way of knowing whether the *Ranger* received it."

"I hope it got through," you say. "What's the present date?"

"We've reentered at the nearest time possible, April 22, 1975."

"Still over Vladivostok?"

"Of course, Inspector. No need to escape to another place when we can escape to another time."

"I'm surprised we had to resort to such an extreme measure," you say, "but since we did, let's set down anyway. Maybe we'll find the answer to the riddle in 1975."

Your computron responds by sending the *Voyager* into a deep descent. A few moments later the craft decelerates sharply; then you feel a little bump and you know that you've landed.

You look out the window. It's pitch-dark and raining. "Where did we land, Chin Chin?"

"At the end of a fishing pier in Vladivostok, Russia's main Pacific port."

"Good work, Chin Chin—I'm on my way." You shut down your computron, strap on your backpack, and exit through the hatch.

It's not only rainy, it's very foggy. You can't see a thing through the mists as you look out toward the harbor. All that's visible are fishing boats in their slips on either side of the pier.

You listen a moment to the water lapping against the boats, and glance at your watch. By now Tang should have landed in Moscow. People there will be just finishing lunch. Yet here in Vladivostok it's past eight o'clock in the evening. People will soon be going to bed.

Suddenly you realize that you haven't yet transformed the *Voyager*. With the power of Turoc, you rearrange its molecules into those of pilings that look as if they were put in to strengthen the pier. Then you start toward the shore.

Turn to page 24.

A few hundred miles above the earth's surface, you bid Tang good-bye, promising to meet him at the statue of Lenin in Novosibirsk in exactly sixty days.

You're preparing for landing and have descended to about twenty miles above the earth's surface when a warning light flashes on.

"Chin Chin, what's happening?"

"Soviet radar picked us up. I had to engage our stealth gear to throw them off. They have very strong air defenses around Moscow."

"I thought that Earthlings weren't advanced enough to detect us, even without our stealth shield," you say.

"That was my data too—*Missiles converging!*" These words from Chin Chin are almost drowned out by a high-pitched whine as the *Voyager* accelerates.

At the same moment these words come upon the screen:

HIT 93.2% CERTAIN!

"Chin Chin," you yell. "Emergency transit!"

You feel a little shudder, then all is calm again; your spacecraft has steadied on course as if nothing had happened!

"We have performed a time evasion," Chin Chin says calmly. "The automatic signal went out, advising the *Ranger*, but I can't be sure it was received."

"We'll just have to hope it was," you say. "What time is it now?"

"About noon, April 22, 1975," your computron replies. "It was the nearest time to the present available."

"Are we still over Moscow?"

"That's right, Inspector. With a time evasion there's no need to escape to another place."

"In this case I'm not so sure," you say. "Let's set down anyway. Maybe we'll find the answer to the riddle in 1975!"

Your computron responds by sending the *Voyager* into a steep descent. A few moments later the craft decelerates sharply; then you feel a little bump. You've landed in a remote section of Gorky Park near the center of Moscow.

You exit through the hatch and quickly transform the *Voyager* into a statue of a factory worker and a plaque to go with it. The plaque says, "Hero of Labor and Industry." From what you learned about Russia on Turoc, you know the statue will be perfectly safe.

Though it's already well into spring, the weather is still very cold, even for Moscow! The paths have been flooded and iced over, and

people are ice-skating, instead of walking, through the park. You wish you had skates!

After leaving the park you walk past a palace with a hammer-and-sickle banner draped over it. Then you pass the Space Monument—a fantastic sculpture that curves as it rises hundreds of feet, just as a rocket might curve on its way into space. At last you reach Red Square and the Kremlin.

You look up at the government buildings. A huge red banner with a picture of Lenin on it is hanging from one of the larger ones. Red banners are flying all over the square. A crowd is forming. There's apparently going to be a celebration—it's Lenin's birthday!

You are watching the festivities when you feel a heavy hand on your shoulder, and you look around at the stern face of a policeman.

"Let me see your papers," he says.

"What papers?"

"Don't joke with me. I can tell you're one of those people who's trying to stay in Moscow more than three days."

You soon learn that only residents of Moscow and privileged citizens are allowed to visit the capital for more than three days. You're in trouble, all right, but there's a thick crowd around you, and you're bioformed to be a fast runner. You squeeze between two portly women and then

break into a sprint, weaving and darting through the crowd until you know you've shaken the cop.

You've gone several blocks and entered a plaza across from a splendid building that looks like a Greek temple. You start to check your map to see where you are. Then you hear a woman's voice behind you.

"Ah, a tourist. Hoping to see the Bolshoi Theater? It's closed now, but perhaps you can come back tomorrow."

You turn to look at her. She has a round, full face with dimples on her cheeks. Her hair is tied up in a bun.

"Yes, I am a tourist," you say. "And I find all these buildings fascinating, but—perhaps you could help me."

"Do you need directions?"

"Not exactly, but tell me—have you ever heard of the Golden Horde?"

"Why yes," she replies. "The Golden Horde— I think—" She looks nervously around. "I must go now." Suddenly she is walking rapidly away!

A moment later you see why—a carload of policemen is pulling up beside you. One of them is the same cop who tried to arrest you a few minutes ago. He leaps out of the car and grabs your arms in a hammerlock. "You're in real trouble now," he says. "We're turning you over to the KGB."

A half hour later you're led into a huge concrete-slab building with no windows on the lower floors. The KGB must have been waiting for you, because an orderly is waiting to meet you. He looks like an Olympic weight lifter. You're afraid he's going to break a bone as he grabs your arm, and he keeps a tight grip on you as he ushers you down a long corridor and shows you into an interrogation room.

An agent looks up at you from the other side of a highly polished desk.

Turn to page 53.

Your backpack contains some Nutra-Max bars and warm clothing, including a fleecy wool hat and extra-warm gloves. Russia is not only the largest country on Earth—it's also the coldest. Though you've arrived in the middle of April, much of the country is still covered with snow.

It's raining, not snowing, in Vladivostok, but you're getting cold and wet, and you're tired after your long trip. Thanks to Simbar's planning, you've brought along a supply of rubles, the national currency, and you decide to spend a few of them tonight for a hotel room. In the morning, you'll begin looking for clues to your riddle.

As you walk past the boats, some fishermen, working on their rig under a floodlight, look up at you.

"*Dobriy vyehchyeer*—good evening," you say.

"*Dobriy vyehchyeer!*" they all reply.

Soon you reach the rain-soaked street that runs past the pier. A van and several trucks pass by, sending up sheets of water from a puddle that goes halfway across the road.

You look up and down for some sign of a hotel. There are lights in both directions, but you

can't see far through the mists. A policeman is coming toward you—maybe he can give you directions.

"Hello," you say, smiling, though he has a stern look on his face.

"Let me see your papers," he demands.

"What papers?"

He jabs a nightstick into your ribs, not hard enough to hurt you, but enough so you decide you better be careful.

"Don't joke with me." He says something into his walkie-talkie. "Your papers," he says again.

"I don't have any," you say. "I'm a Russian." (You feel it's fair to say this, because you've been bioformed to look and talk like a Russian.)

"I can tell you're a Russian! That's why you should know enough to hand over your papers."

Just then a van pulls up. Two more policemen jump out. Without a word, they make you climb into the back. They slam the door behind you, and the van rumbles off. You have to sit down in a hurry to keep from losing your balance while it careens through the rain-soaked streets of the city.

A few minutes later you're in jail.

Turn to page 94.

For the next few days, you have no company at all in your cell as you wait for your plane ride to Moscow. Then one morning you are awakened early by a guard shaking your shoulder. "Come!" he barks at you. "The plane leaves in forty minutes!"

You grab your backpack and take a last look around at the bare cinder-block walls. Twenty minutes later, in the early gloomy light of another misty day, you arrive at the airport in a van exactly like the one that brought you from the pier. A guard escorts you into a low concrete building with the Soviet emblem, a hammer and sickle, painted on its front. Inside, you wait on a bench in a big, overheated room crowded with travelers, most of them sailors and naval officers. Your KGB guard sits across from you, reading his copy of *Pravda*, the government newspaper.

A ruddy-faced woman comes by, wheeling a food cart. For fifty kopecks—half a ruble—you get a stale roll, a pickle, and some tea.

The KGB man keeps looking at you over the top of his newspaper. You're sure he has a gun. Not that you want to escape. You've decided

you're more likely to learn about the Golden Horde by talking to officials in Moscow.

After hours of delay, the plane finally takes off. It's hardly off the ground when the clouds close in around it—you can barely see the tips of the wings.

Yuri, the stocky, pink-faced KGB agent sitting next to you, tells you that your flight to Moscow will take ten hours, counting a short layover in Novosibirsk. This is, of course, the same city where you'd hoped to meet Tang.

Yuri seems very proud of how big Russia is. "The distance from Vladivostok to Moscow," he says, "is about the same as from Seattle to Tokyo, or from New York to Hawaii. In fact," he adds, "the United States would have to extend almost halfway across the North Pacific to be as big as the Soviet Union."

He also tells you that, even though Canada is the world's second-largest country and that the United States is the third-largest country, the Soviet Union is a good deal bigger than both of them combined.

You don't want to hear this kind of thing for ten hours, so you decide to change the subject to one *you* want to talk about. "Tell me, Yuri," you say, "have you ever heard of the Golden Horde?"

The KGB man looks puzzled but seems anxious to show how much he knows. "That sounds like an army," he says. "Maybe it was the army of Hitler that invaded Russia in 1940. Though Hitler and our leader Stalin had just promised to live in peace with each other, Hitler sent his tanks onto our noble soil. Our people were alone. They had almost no help from the capitalist countries. Yet they heroically resisted the enemy. Millions of Russians died, but we destroyed most of Hitler's armies and beat the rest of them back through the gates of Berlin!" Yuri is puffed up with pride. He has completely forgotten that you were asking about the Golden Horde.

You know that most of what Yuri said is true. The Russians did fight back bravely, despite terrible suffering and losses. But you also know that Yuri went to a school controlled by the Communist party. He may not know that Stalin made a peace pact with Hitler, not because Stalin loved peace but so the two of them could divide the country of Poland between them!

Yuri talks on and on, but he finally stops when a steward comes down the aisle with a meal of soup, cucumbers, and black bread.

You're amazed at how hungry Yuri is. He finishes his soup in no time. You leave yours—you don't think your stomach could take it if the plane were to run into bumpy air. You feel like snatching a Turonian Nutra-Max bar from your backpack but decide you better save them.

Soon afterward there's a break in the clouds and you can finally see the ground below. It looks rugged and parched, with splotches of snow on the mountains.

"We're crossing Chinese air space," Yuri says. "That's the northern tip of Manchuria."

You sleep awhile; then an hour or so later Yuri nudges you awake. "That's Lake Baykal," he says, pointing out the window. "It's three hundred miles long and a mile deep and has more water in it than all the Great Lakes of America!"

You look down at this vast body of water, extending north and south as far as you can see. It's almost completely frozen, though it's now late April. You wonder when it will thaw.

You sleep most of the next two hours, and land in Novosibirsk in a snowstorm. You're tired of flying and rather unhappy when Yuri tells you that Moscow is still a three-hour flight away—about the same as from Chicago to San Francisco.

Ten minutes later you learn that your plane has been grounded because of engine problems. Yuri tells you that he'll take you to the local KGB headquarters for the night.

The two of you walk through the airport terminal, which is jammed with people milling around and sleeping on benches. Outside the entrance a KGB car is waiting to pick you up.

You hear Yuri talking to the driver. A high-level KGB official is in town, and he is going to question you. You won't have to go to Moscow!

On the way into the city you're driven past clusters of log cabins. Then suddenly you're passing rows of nine-story-high concrete apartments—dozens of them that all look alike. A few minutes later you peer eagerly through the window as you pass the Opera and Ballet Theater and notice a huge statue of Lenin. It's the very place you were going to meet Tang!

When you reach the KGB building, Yuri shows you to your room, which is not a bedroom actually, but a tiny office with a cot along one wall. Hanging over the cot is a small picture of Lenin.

Yuri leaves you there, but almost immediately another man comes, bringing a Russian pastry called blini—with caviar and sour cream beside it and, on a separate dish, sturgeon, and cakes on the side!

You try some. As the Russians say, it's *plokhah*—good!

Food like this is a rarity in Russia except for important people, and you're amazed to be getting such treatment. They must be trying to soften you up by giving you a good meal.

That suspicion is confirmed when Yuri returns with a smiling, puffy-faced man wearing a couple of dozen medals on his chest.

"I am Colonel Smyslov," the man says cheerfully. "I am the one you can talk to—the one you *must* talk to."

You merely nod—you'll see what questions he asks.

Smyslov looks at you carefully, moving from side to side to inspect you from different angles. "I have never seen a spy who spoke such good Russian, but wasn't Russian," he says presently, "and I do know you are *not* Russian. There is something a little different about the way you look and the way you talk. Perhaps your father was a diplomat here, or a journalist, and you attended our schools?"

"No," you answer. "I've never been in Russia before."

Smyslov edges closer. He shoves a pudgy finger into your chest. "Don't try to evade me. You will regret it very much if you don't cooperate."

These people will wear you down sooner or later, you think. As far as you can see, you might as well tell them you're an Earth Inspector. It won't really violate the Earth Inspector code, because they will never believe what you say!

Yet maybe that's not such a good idea. Maybe you should tell him something else—that you're an American journalist, for instance, and that you lost your passport.

If you tell Colonel Smyslov that you're an Earth Inspector, turn to page 42.

If you say you're an American journalist, turn to page 45.

The next morning you're awakened early and taken to the railroad station.

Dimitri, the KGB agent guarding you, marches you along the platform. "You'll be riding on the Trans-Siberian Railroad, the longest rail line in the world," he says. "It's eight thousand miles—nine days—to Moscow, but of course, you won't be going that far. You're going to the prison compound near Irkutsk on the shores of Lake Baykal in Siberia."

He shoves you into a car half filled with prisoners who are lined up on hard benches on either side of the aisle. An armed guard stands at each end.

"You sit on the bench the whole way," Dimitri tells you. "Prisoners are allowed to go to the bathroom one at a time. Food and water will be brought twice a day. Don't count on the good treatment you received in Vladivostok."

You find a spot on one of the benches and sit down as the train lurches into motion.

All that day the train rumbles across the countryside, most of it hilly and thickly forested. It's a dismal ride. The other prisoners have little to

say. They look as if they've lost hope. At least the guards seem quite relaxed. They let you lie down on the floor and sleep when you want to.

All day long the train chugs along. At dusk you reach a fairly large city called Khabarovsk.

You sleep fitfully that night. In the morning you look out and see that it's snowing. The train is moving steadily through the *taiga*, the vast northern forest.

During the morning, you strike up a conversation with another prisoner. His name is Anton Goldofsky. He tells you that he worked on a collective farm and that he was caught selling tomatoes on the black market. He's been sentenced to ten years working in an aluminum smelter in northern Siberia.

"Northern Siberia has many resources," Anton says. "Not only lumber, but also oil, gas, metals, and minerals. Not many people want to live there. In winter the temperature rarely rises above twenty below zero, and even in the summer the ground never thaws."

"I've heard that it's been a tradition in Russia to send prisoners to work in Siberia," you say.

Anton nods. "Yes. That was true long before the Communists came to power. One of our great writers, Fyodor Dostoyevsky, was imprisoned in Siberia by one of the czars."

"Anton, have you ever heard of the Golden Horde?"

He squints at you, thinking. "It sounds familiar. It may have had something to do with one of the first czars, Ivan the Terrible."

You tell Anton how you happened to be arrested. "I don't think they will sentence me to hard labor," you say. "Unlike you, I committed no crime."

"No crime?" He gives a little laugh. "You are a possible spy. That's a worse crime than mine."

"Don't they have to *prove* I'm a spy?"

Anton shakes his head. "Look, it's only natural they were suspicious. I'm suspicious myself. What *were* you doing on that pier in Vladivostok, and where do you come from, anyway?"

You start to say something, but Anton raises a hand. "That's all right—it's none of my business."

You lean close and whisper. "Tell me, Anton, is there any way we can escape?"

"Would you want to escape into that?" he asks, pointing toward the bleak, snowy forest passing by.

At this point your spirits sink very low. You feel you've been failing in your mission from the moment you landed. If only you'd never left Turoc. Everyone there told you that only the smartest and boldest of the Turonians were chosen to be Earth Inspectors. Now you're beginning to think that only the dumbest and craziest were.

You wonder how Tang is doing, and whether you'll ever see him again.

You have another fitful night's sleep on the floor. It's only about 4:00 a.m. when you awaken. There's a dull, hazy glow in the east. The sun will be up in about an hour. The guard at the end of the car lets you by so you can go to the lavatory. While you're there, the train lurches to a stop. As you come out, you see that the guard has stepped out onto the platform between the cars. You watch him climb down to the bottom step. At that moment you hear the sound of a chain saw from the front of the train.

You hear the guard yelling. "Hey—why did we stop?"

Someone calls, "They have to clear away a tree that fell on the tracks!"

It's now or never, you tell yourself. You run to the side of the platform, opposite the guard, and jump! He never hears you as you land in the soft snow. It's too deep to walk through—you'd be exhausted after a few hundred yards. No wonder they're not worried about prisoners escaping! Even if you could walk, where would you go? There could be fifty miles of forest between you and the next road. Just the same, you're determined not to get back on that train.

You tunnel into the snow so you won't be seen. In a few minutes you hear the *chug, chug,*

chug of the train moving forward. You dig your way out in time to see the last cars disappearing around the bend.

You climb up to the roadbed, which has been cleared of all but a few inches of snow, and start walking along the tracks. The sun will be up soon. The temperature may even rise above freezing. You eat half a Nutra-Max bar and feel much better—until you remember that you're in Siberia. Your map shows no roads or towns until you get to Ulan Ude, which must be at least a hundred miles to the west. Long before that, night will fall, and the bitter cold will return. You walk faster, though you know it's not going to make much difference.

Turn to page 103.

42

"All right, I'll tell the truth," you say. "I'm an Earth Inspector. I've come from the planet Turoc to find out certain things about your world."

Smyslov interrupts you with a belly laugh. "Oh, ho, ho—and where have you parked your spaceship?" he says.

"That," you say, "I cannot tell you."

"Of course, of course," Smyslov says with mock seriousness. Then his tone changes sharply. "Yuri—we have a mental patient on our hands. Take this 'Earth Inspector' to the Melankoff Hospital for the Insane."

"Hey, I'm not insane," you say loudly. "And I'm peaceful."

Smyslov edges closer. You shrink back, but he speaks in a soft, gentle voice. "It's for your own good, comrade—for your own good."

A few minutes later, you're locked in the back of a van, which races down a side street, turns onto a major road, and starts over a bridge. Through the metal netting in the back, you can see that you're crossing the Ob, the great river that rises in the Altai Mountains on the Chinese border. Even though it's late April, the river is

still clogged with huge chunks of ice, which, since they are headed toward the Arctic Ocean, may never melt.

Turn to page 62.

"The truth is," you say, "I'm an American journalist. I wanted to travel everywhere in Russia and write about it so our people would understand it better. I have no interest in your military preparations."

Smyslov laughs. "That's a story we hear all the time. We know you're a spy—and a big one. We're going to fly you to Moscow. Our highest-ranking interrogators want to talk to you, and I'll tell you right now, they won't accept any phony stories from you. You're going to tell the truth!"

You must be a pretty high priority case, because they have you on the plane in half an hour. In only four hours you're in KGB headquarters in Moscow, sitting across a desk from another agent. The room is much larger and better furnished than the one in Novosibirsk. It has a red carpet and several large chairs. The desk is made of beautifully finished mahogany, and the picture of Lenin on the wall has a gilt-edged frame.

Turn to page 53.

"I'd rather try to escape," you tell Pytor. "Good." He pats your shoulder. "If I were younger, I'd try myself, but—anyway, here's the plan. One of the guards—his name is Igor—owes me a favor. I once saved his father from the KGB. Tomorrow night he is on the midnight to eight a.m. shift. I'll get word to him to let you out through the gate just before dawn. Wait by the side of the road by the sign pointing to the hospital. Igor's brother, Mikhail, is a truck driver who happens to be leaving with a shipment of electric motors early tomorrow. His destination is Tomsk, which is about a hundred and twenty miles northeast of Novosibirsk. Igor will arrange for Mikhail to pick you up exactly at sunrise and take you with him to as far as you want to go. From then on you're on your own."

You thank Pytor and bid him farewell. That night you sleep in your clothes. Shortly before dawn, Igor awakens you. You follow him as he silently unlocks the door of the ward and leads you down a staircase. A night watchman is passing by just as you reach the lobby. You throw up your hands as he reaches for his gun.

Igor grabs your arm. "It's all right—I know this man. You have only to make him a small gift." To the night watchman he says, "Mischa—let's pretend you were patrolling at the other end of the building. My friend here has something for you, by the way." He nudges you.

The watchman approaches. "What have you got? It better not be a knife."

You realize you have to give him a bribe, but what? There's only one possibility. You reach in your backpack and pull out one of the Nutra-Max bars that you brought from Turoc. Though they have more vitamins than any Earth food, they taste even better than chocolate—better than anything! You hold one out to the watchman. He takes it and looks at it suspiciously. You pull out another and break off a piece and eat it. "Try it," you say.

The watchman bites off a piece. He smiles. "Good—very good!" he says. "I will inspect the other end of the building."

"Hurry," Igor tells you. "It's almost sunrise." He unlocks a door leading outside and points to where you are to wait for his brother. "Good luck," he says.

"Thanks, Igor." You hand him a Nutra-Max bar—it seems the least you can do, though you now have only three left.

Turn to page 72.

You decide to wait, thinking that if you escape, you'll probably be caught again anyway.

The next day Pytor is transferred to another ward. No one else is as friendly, so it gets pretty lonely for you. Psychiatrists come to interview you several times, no doubt hoping you'll admit you're a spy. After a week one of them tells you that you'll be released. You feel like jumping with joy until he tells you that all your rubles have been confiscated. "Everything belongs to the state," he says, "especially money you can't explain how you got." The psychiatrist insists that you are very lucky, though: You will be issued a new internal passport and given a job as a clerk at the GUM, the big government-run department store in Moscow. This doesn't sound bad, but then you find out that you will have to share a small apartment with four other people. Housing is in scarce supply in the overcrowded capital city, and everyone has to make do.

When you start your new job, you learn that most of your pay will have to go for food and rent—it will be very hard to save any money. To save as much as possible, you even walk to work,

choosing a route that takes you over a bridge where you can get a good view of the river traffic and the Moscow skyline. However, you have another problem: Because of your curious situation, you were issued a passport that does not allow you to travel outside of Moscow. At least your job is quite pleasant, and you like nearly everyone you meet. The Russians are wonderful people, you decide.

GUM is an enormous store, and you learn that people come long distances to shop there. Nonetheless, many goods are in short supply. Some sales booths are almost deserted because they are stocked with poorly made yet expensive goods. Others are very busy, with long lines of customers waiting to get to the counters. You learn that this always happens when a shipment of scarce merchandise arrives.

Your job is to unpack goods and then wheel them to the sales booths and help the clerks place them on the shelves. Life could be worse. As a suspected spy, you could have been sent to work in a lead mine in Siberia or something like that. On the other hand, you feel trapped. After two weeks' work you've made only thirty rubles. That's not nearly enough for a ticket to Novosibirsk. It would barely take you as far as Gorky, a city 500 miles east of Moscow.

You're really discouraged. No one you've talked to in Moscow has heard of the Golden

Horde. Your spacecraft is stuck at the other end of the country, 8000 miles away, and your only hope of finding Tang is to go to Novosibirsk, almost 2500 miles beyond Gorky, and even then he won't be there if he didn't get Chin Chin's message about your time displacement.

Despite these problems, you're determined to get started on your trip. You could take the train as far as Gorky, but maybe you should hitchhike and save the little money you have.

If you take a subway to the edge of the city and try to hitch a ride to Novosibirsk, turn to page 10.

If you use your eight rubles to take the train to Gorky, turn to page 65.

This agent is a man in his sixties with a full head of steel-gray hair. He is wearing an expensive three-piece suit, a maroon eye patch, and a matching silk necktie. He glares at you with a single, piercing blue eye.

"Tell us the truth," he says. "You're a spy, aren't you?"

"I am *not* a spy—I'm a journalist."

The agent regards you suspiciously. He turns and walks out of the room, leaving a policeman to stand watch. You wait for what seems like forever before he comes back.

"I have discussed your case with the deputy director of the KGB," he tells you. "Since there is no evidence against you, we are going to let you go."

"Well, thanks, I'm glad," you say, but your smile fades as he points a finger uncomfortably close to your nose.

"Just remember—the law in this country is very important. If you do anything illegal, you will feel the weight of justice on your shoulders." Saying this, the agent presses his hand on your shoulder. You can feel its weight.

You feel like smacking him one; instead, you say, "I understand."

A few minutes later you're free, for the moment at least.

You stroll through Red Square and gaze up at the fantastic onion domes of St. Basil's Cathedral, now a museum. You pass Lenin's tomb. Two soldiers stand stiffly at attention at the entrance. A long line of people are waiting to view Lenin's body, which lies inside, displayed in a glass-topped case.

You become aware of someone watching you. Though you have an Earthling body, you have more sensitivity than most Earthlings because you're so used to receiving thought waves on Turoc. You decide to walk in a random fashion and see if this person follows you.

You walk through the grounds of the Kremlin, the huge, ancient fortress that is now the seat of Soviet government, and stroll past palaces dating from the times of the czars. You sense that the man is still tailing you, and you realize why you were let free. Instead of trying to force information from you, the KGB has decided to let you lead them to your contacts!

You leave the Kremlin and walk rapidly through GUM, the huge state-run department store, hoping to shake the man following you. The store is jammed with shoppers, and you duck

in and out of lines of people lined up in front of the sales stalls, but you can't shake the KGB man.

You leave the store and turn down a side street. A huge billboard above you says, "BUILD SOCIALISM." Ahead of you is another long line of people. You walk toward the head of the line, which winds around a corner. Ahead of you is the Moscow State Theater. The people in this line must be trying to get tickets to a concert. You've learned that culture is very important to the Soviet people.

You see an opening and cut through. Near the head of the line, someone is arguing with the ticket-taker. You don't want to sneak into the theater, but this is an emergency! You dart inside and walk quickly along behind the back row. The theater is already filled, and many people are standing in the rear. You slip among them, hoping the KGB man didn't see where you went. A few seconds later the house lights dim, the curtain goes up, and the orchestra begins to play.

For the next two hours you completely forget that you're an Earth Inspector—you're so fascinated by the wonderful dancers and the beautiful music. At the end of each scene the audience cheers and claps, and for good reason! The music is by the great Russian composer Prokofiev, and the dancers belong to one of the most famous companies in the world—the Bolshoi Ballet.

Never before have you seen such a great performance, even on Turoc!

A few minutes later, as you walk out of the theater with the music still ringing in your ears, you feel a hand on your shoulder. You wheel around and stare into the grim face of a policeman.

"Sneaking into a theater—that was a very foolish thing to do," he says. Later, in KGB headquarters, you hear the same words from a junior officer. A moment later the same agent who talked to you before—the one with the maroon eye patch—walks in.

"No, Popov," he says to the younger man. "It was *not* a foolish thing to do. It was a *crazy* thing to do." He rests a hand on your shoulder. "It is obvious now that you need special attention. Tomorrow we shall fly you to Siberia. You'll get the treatment you need at the Melankoff Mental Hospital."

Turn to page 62.

Though it's mid-May, a chill north wind is whipping through the streets of Novosibirsk. You are standing near the statue of Lenin outside the Opera and Ballet Theater, wishing the sun would come out from behind a cloud. You've been waiting there for hours, hoping that Tang got Chin Chin's message about your time evasion, and has journeyed back to the year 1975 himself. If he hasn't, you'll have to get back to your spacecraft in Vladivostok on your own, and that won't be easy. You'll just have to hope he shows up. It's just about your only hope, because you're still more than three thousand miles from Vladivostok and you have hardly a ruble left to your name.

After a several-hour wait, you feel a tap on the shoulder. You turn and look into the eyes of a young Russian woman.

"My name is Olga—do you need work?" she asks.

"How did you guess?" you ask.

"I can tell—when someone wants to work outside the system." She holds out her hand and you shake it.

"The only thing," she says, "is that you'll have to work in the evening."

"That's fine," you say, thinking that during the daytime you can come back to the square where you were to meet Tang. That way you won't miss him if he comes.

The job Olga got for you is working in a furniture factory. The reason you work in the evening is that the factory is owned by the government, like nearly everything else, but in the evening the manager and certain workers, like Olga, make extra furniture, which they sell privately on the black market. You learn that many people make extra money in such ways, though it's illegal.

Turn to page 99.

Before darkness falls the next day, you're in your new home in the Melankoff Hospital, somewhere in western Siberia, trying to figure out why you were brought there. You're sitting on a narrow cot in a ward of a hospital that's very different from most hospitals. Every one of its windows is barred.

You cast your eyes around at the other patients (or prisoners—you're not sure how to think of them). A few of them look rather crazy, but most of them look perfectly sane. Several are playing chess.

A man with a time-worn face and snow white hair looks up from the book he is reading. "Ah, I can see you're a dissident like me," he says. "My name is Pytor. Don't worry, I won't ask you any questions, not even your name. I understand you have no way of knowing whether I may be an informer."

"In any event I'm glad to meet you," you say. "In what way are you a dissident?"

"I've written articles in which I argued that our leaders should be elected by popular vote."

"I hope that someday that will be possible," you say.

"Exactly." Pytor puts down his book and gestures at you with his glasses. "Spoken like a true dissident. That is to say, you are not afraid to speak the truth."

"But why do they put a dissident in a mental hospital?"

"It's one of their methods for making people conform. It's embarrassing for them to put too many people in jail. They find it useful to treat some people, like me and you, by calling them mentally ill. They pretend to try to cure a disease we don't have. The cure consists of our convincing them we will follow the party line."

"But I thought that conditions had improved in Russia," you say.

"They have," Pytor says. "If Stalin were still ruling the country, you would probably have been shot by now, or committed to slave labor in Siberia, which in my opinion is worse!"

You walk over to Pytor and speak very softly, lest the hospital ward is bugged. "Have you ever heard of the Golden Horde?"

Pytor rubs his forehead a moment, thinking. "Let's see, the Golden Horde—I wish I could remember—My mind is not what it once was. *Wait—now I remember. It had to do with an invading army—I think in the time of Peter the Great.*"

"Pytor." You lean close to the old man. "Is there any way I can get out of here?"

"There are two possibilities," Pytor whispers. "You can wait, and follow all the rules, and say what they want you to say, and after a few months they will probably get tired of you and decide you're not such a threat after all, and let you go. Or you can try to escape. If you want to take the risk, I'll tell you a way that has a chance of success. But I must warn you. If you don't succeed, you'll probably end up in a prison in which you'll spend the rest of your days."

If you attempt to escape, turn to page 46.

If you decide to wait it out, turn to page 48.

When you reach the railroad station you find there's a train leaving for Gorky in just two minutes. You're the last one to climb aboard, but fortunately you're able to find a seat.

Your journey takes you across an open plateau, past farms and wooded lands and factories belching forth smoke. Natasha, the young woman sitting next to you, strikes up a conversation. Though she is not able to give you any clues about the Golden Horde, you soon make friends with her. Naturally she asks why you're going to Gorky. You decide to take a chance and tell her that you are trying to meet a friend in Novosibirsk, though your internal passport does not allow you to travel outside of Moscow.

At that moment she nudges your shoulder and points toward the rear of the car. "Look, here comes the conductor. It's not enough that you have a ticket—he'll demand to see your passport. Your only hope is to hide in the lavatory at the forward end of the car. He'll come through just once, and if he misses you, you'll be all right."

"Thanks." You watch until the conductor is facing away from you, arguing with a passenger about something, and then you hurry forward

and lock yourself in the lavatory. The conductor must have a key, of course—you just have to hope he doesn't check.

You jam yourself into a little niche next to a fire extinguisher, and wait and wait, afraid to come out, not knowing whether he's gone past yet. Then you shudder as you hear a key turn the latch. The door opens. Out of the corner of your eye, you see the conductor's scarlet jacket. Why did you ever think you could get away with this!

To your amazement he doesn't go to the toilet or check around. Instead, he stands by the window and looks out at the fields and meadows passing by. You wonder what he is thinking. Perhaps he wishes he were not so far from home. That's the way you feel too.

You stand frozen, not daring to breathe. Just as you think the conductor is going to look your way, he returns to the corridor, gripping the door frame to keep from losing his balance as the train passes over a rough stretch of road.

When you return to your seat, Natasha welcomes you with a big smile. "Good going," she says. "He won't be back again—and we'll soon be in Gorky."

Despite your troubles with the KGB you decide that most Russians are friendly, warmhearted people. Feeling free to talk, you tell Natasha how you need to get to Novosibirsk even though you haven't a ruble to your name.

"Your troubles are just beginning," she says. "You will never be able to get a ride on a truck from Gorky. There is a secret military plant east of the city, and the police are checking every vehicle that goes by. Since you have no money, you can't bribe anyone; otherwise you might get through. As for taking the train there, don't think you'll be so lucky hiding in the lavatory next time."

"Then what do you think I should do?"

"You'd have a much better chance stowing away on the steamer going down the Volga. There's one leaving at noon tomorrow. You may sleep at my house tonight. Once you're aboard the ship, offer to help in the kitchen. They are so overworked that they won't ask questions if you agree to mop the floor and do the dishes."

"Where does the steamer go?" you ask.

"South, to where the river empties into the Caspian Sea. But don't stay on that long. When you reach the city of Volgograd, go to this address. It's the home of my brother, Sergei Turgenyev. He will help you reach Novosibirsk."

Thanks to Natasha's help and a bit of luck, you walk off the train at Gorky without a policeman holding you by the arm. And shortly before noon the next day, you board the 300-foot-long steamer, the *Lenin*, and head immediately for the kitchen. Just as Natasha predicted, the staff is glad to have help. In return they let you use an extra bunk in the crew's quarters.

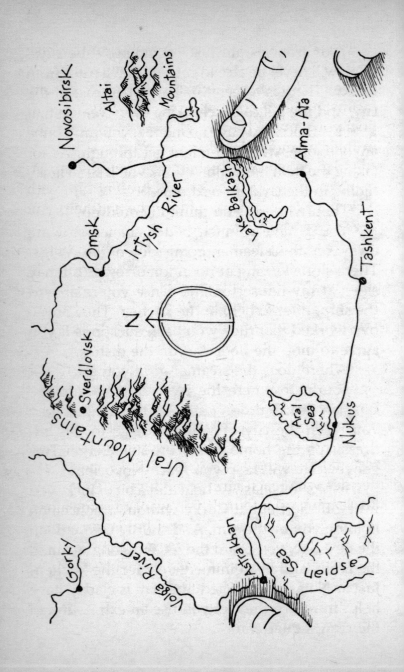

Two days later you reach Volgograd, which used to be called Stalingrad. Here, more than half a million Russians died in defense of the city against Hitler's armies. From the deck of your boat you can see the two gigantic statues erected in their memory.

Once you get off the boat you go to the apartment of Sergei Turgenyev and present him with Natasha's letter and ask him if he can help you get to Novosibirsk.

A tall young man with coal-black hair, Sergei scowls at you fiercely. "My sister knows I would do anything for her, but sometimes I wish she weren't so kindly to others. Yes, I can help you. I'm an agronomist. I travel throughout the country and visit farms and decide what model tractors should be shipped to each one."

"The farmers don't come here to buy the tractors?" you say.

Sergei shakes his head. "No, these are collective farms, all owned by the government, so a representative of the government—in this case me—decides what each farm should have. Tomorrow I'm leaving on a tour. If you want to come along in my truck, you can." Sergei holds out a map for you to look at. "See, I've marked the route we'll be taking. It should take us just about three weeks to reach Novosibirsk."

Turn to page 102.

You're waiting by the side of the road, shivering in the cold morning air. A couple of trucks and a bus go by. You wonder if the sun is up yet. You can't tell because of the line of dark clouds hanging on the horizon. A big trailer truck grinds to a stop. The driver yells down.

"You look like you need a ride. I'm headed for Tomsk, passing through Novosibirsk."

You jump into the cab, and the truck is in motion again before you even shut the door.

The driver holds out his hand for you to shake. "Mikhail is my name," he says. He is a heavy man with a ruddy complexion. You know by the big smile he gives you that you'll like him.

"Thanks for picking me up," you say.

"I like company," Mikhail says. "I drive this truck thousands of miles a week, winter and summer—it gets lonely."

"Where do you go on your trips?"

"Everywhere. I just came from Armenia in the southwestern part of our country, near Turkey. Before that, I was in Leningrad, that beautiful city on the Baltic Sea. And once I went all the way to Yakutsk, near the Arctic Circle in northeastern Siberia. It's so cold there that truckers have to

leave their engines running all winter." He glances at you. "Did you ever try to start an engine when it's sixty below zero?"

You shake your head.

The truck rumbles along the bumpy road.

"Yes," says Mikhail. "I've seen as much of Russia as anybody. And what I've seen in the last few years makes me sad."

"How so?" you ask.

"The environment is being ruined. Waste from mining and manufacturing has polluted our rivers and lakes. Even Lake Baykal, the largest supply of fresh water in the world, is turning bad. And our forests—the greatest in the world—are in danger. Some places where once there was only the scent of pines and larch—now I smell sulfur or coal."

"I've heard this sort of thing is happening all over this planet," you say. Then, remembering your mission, you ask, "Mikhail, in your travels around the Soviet Union, have you ever heard of the Golden Horde?"

Mikhail runs his hand through his tousled black hair. "That phrase is familiar. It might have something to do with the Romanov family—the czars that ruled Russia for hundreds of years."

Mikhail spends the next hour talking about Soviet accomplishments—how the Russians were the first to conquer space, how their hydroelectric dams are the greatest in the world, how great

their athletes are, and how many Olympic medals they've won, and so on, until you fall asleep. When you awaken, the landscape has changed. Instead of endless steppes (what Americans would call prairies) you see nothing but trees. You have entered the *taiga*, that vast region of subarctic forest that stretches six thousand miles across the Soviet Union.

You look over at Mikhail. You can tell he is tired from driving so long. "How close are we to Novosibirsk?" you ask.

"Just a few miles—*oh oh.*" He slams on the brakes. Several trucks are stopped ahead.

"It's a roadblock. They may be looking for you! Jump out fast and run into the woods!"

By the time Mikhail has said this, he's brought the truck to a stop and thrown open your door. *"Hurry!"* He practically shoves you out.

"Thanks for the ride!" you shout as you turn and run. In a few seconds you reach the forest.

You're lucky it's the middle of May. A few weeks ago, the snow would have been too deep to walk through. And further on into spring, flies and mosquitoes could eat you alive. As it is, you're able to walk the three miles remaining to Novosibirsk. The only trouble is that you're arriving there in 1975, years before Tang is due to meet you!

Turn to page 60.

The year is 1718, during the reign of Peter the Great, and you've just landed the *Voyager* on a farm outside of Moscow. Hundreds of years from now, dozens of high-rise apartment buildings will surround this spot. But right now there's nothing in sight but snow-covered pastureland and woods.

You suddenly realize that you failed to tell Chin Chin what month to land in. It's the middle of winter and snowing hard as you step out into the bitter, blustery wind. You'd like to come back in the spring or summer, when there aren't two feet of snow on the ground, but you don't have time for that, and you'd better hide your spacecraft in a hurry. A large sledge, pulled by two horses, is coming across the fields.

You quickly transform the *Voyager* into an old farm wagon, then stand in the knee-deep snow and watch the sledge draw closer. It's stacked high with deer carcasses, no doubt on their way into Moscow. You run up as the sledge comes by. It's driven by an old man wrapped in furs, his face lined by decades of toil and weather. You call to him, "Can you give me a ride into the city?"

The old man reins in the horses; the sledge draws to a halt. He looks down at you suspiciously.

"You'd freeze if I didn't," he says in a hoarse voice. "There's a blizzard making up."

As if by signal, the wind starts to blow harder, and the snow flies more thickly.

You climb aboard the sledge and pull your parka tightly around your neck. You study the man's face. He must be almost eighty years old. And he must have seen a great deal of history pass by. Perhaps he knows of the Golden Horde.

The old man stares at you until you look away, then he makes a loud, throaty sound and applies his stick to the backs of the horses. The sledge jerks forward.

"Have you heard what the czar's done?" he shouts to you over the wind.

"No," you yell back.

"He's laying a tax on the head of every peasant—making them even poorer than they were. It was bad enough when he taxed each household."

The snow swirls around the sledge, driving at you like fine needles. You brush it away from your eyes. "Why is he doing that?"

"Drat! I can't see—this snow's so thick," the old man yells. "I'm not even sure I'm on the road!"

You peer through the raging snowstorm. It's a blur of white everywhere you look. The old man's eyebrows and beard are covered with frost. Snow lies thickly on his fur wraps.

"What was that you asked?" the driver yells.

"Why is the czar taxing the peasants so much?"

"Because of his wars with the Swedes and the Turks," he shouts in a hoarse, croaking voice. "He's driven foreigners out of Russia, but he makes the peasants bleed for it!"

The roaring wind drowns out his next words. You shiver and pull your parka tighter still.

The driver cups his hand close to your ear. "They call him Peter the Great, but I call him Peter the Terrible!"

At that moment you hear a long, low cry from somewhere behind the sledge. It rises in pitch, then falls off. You hear another, and another—the last one closer.

The horses whinny as they plunge through the deepening snow.

The old man leans close to you, and you feel his breath on your cheek. *Wolves,* he mutters, and hits his horses with a long stick and hits them again until you grab his arm.

"They can't go faster!" you shout.

He stares at you—there's a wild look in his eyes. He lets the reins fall from his hands, and shouts. *"Things are no better than they were in the days of the Golden Horde!"*

You clutch his shoulder. *"What did you say— tell me more!"*

AOOOOUUUU! AOOOOOUUUU! The wolves are suddenly close by!

"They'll make a meal of us!" the old man yells in his croaking voice. *"Ha ha!"* He laughs wildly. *"They think they have as much right to our flesh as we have to their pelts!"*

The reins have dropped from the old man's hands. You take them up and urge the horses on, but they seem exhausted, barely able to move through the drifts.

You've never been so scared, but you yell, *"What was the Golden Horde?"*

"The Mongols—" As he says this, the old man tilts forward. He gasps. You try to prop him up, but he slumps to the side. You turn his head and look into his eyes, which are fixed in a glassy stare. You pat his face, trying to bring him to, as the blizzard whirls about the sledge and snow gathers on his beard.

As if they know their work will be easier for them, the wolves howl more loudly still. One of them, huge and shaggy, lopes close alongside. The horses rear up and plunge their hooves deep into the snow. The old man is dead, and you soon will be too, of that you are sure.

A dark shape appears in the veil of snow before you. Is it a vision of death? No—it's an old farm wagon half buried in the snow! The horses plunge toward it, and your heart leaps. It's the *Voyager!* You've been traveling in a circle and come back to where you started!

You bring the sledge to a halt and cut loose the horses. Freed from their traces, they race through the snow with the wolves in pursuit. You gently wrap the poor old man in his furs. You wish there was something else you could do, but the rule is strict—not to interfere.

You transform the wagon back into your spacecraft and leap inside. A few seconds later you're off the ground, streaking through the snow-filled clouds.

"Chin Chin?" you ask, "do you have any data about the Mongols?"

Go on to the next page.

As you pass through the stratosphere, you see the *Ranger* swooping in alongside you.

"Glad to see you," Tang radios. "*A-chooo!* Excuse me, I think I'm coming down with one of those colds Earthlings tend to get. I had a rough time in the court of Catherine the Great. Her secret police almost packed me away to the iron mines. I thought I would be safe during her reign because I learned that she was reforming the government, and had decreed that the courts, the legislature, and the executive would all be independent of one another."

"That's the way it was set up in America," you say.

"Yeah, but there was a big difference in Russia," Tang says. "Catherine decided that, no matter how things were set up, she would remain in charge of everything!"

"Well, I had quite a time too," you say. "And I think I've learned the answer to the riddle—or most of it."

You tell him the sad story about the old man and what he said about the Golden Horde. Just then Chin Chin's data comes up on the screen.

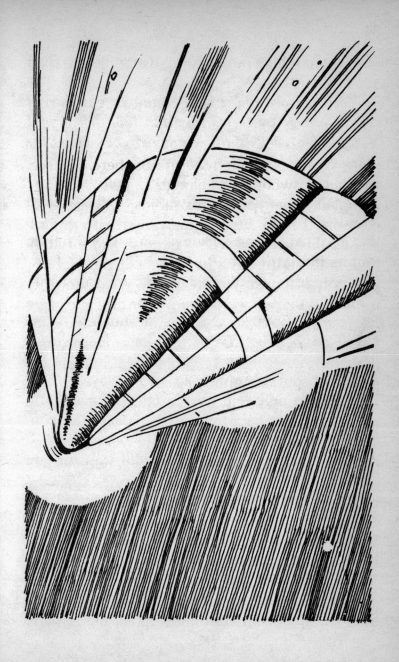

You patch it into Tang's computer so he can read it too.

The Mongols, under Batu Khan, the grandson of Ghengis Khan, conquered Russia in 1237. They ruled the land for more than two hundred years before the Russians were able to drive them out.

"If I'm not mistaken, Tang," you say, "the Mongols who conquered Russia were the Golden Horde."

"That's it!" Tang exclaims. "But why did they call them that?"

"Search the word 'golden' in your data bank, Chin Chin."

Your computron answers a moment later. *"Only one reference: The Mongol leader had a golden tent."*

"That sounds impossible," Tang says.

"There's only one way to tell for sure," you say. "I'm going back through the space–time continuum and check this out."

Tang sneezes again. "I think I'll wait for you here."

"It shouldn't take me long," you say. "Chin Chin, prepare to transit—we'll reenter the space–time continuum in Earth year 1257."

The *Voyager* performs flawlessly. You've hardly had time to check your data file before you're gliding over Siberia, then crossing the Ural Mountains into Europe. Your craft slows, and soon you're low enough to see herds of deer grazing on the long, tufted grass.

In all this vast expanse of what will someday be the Soviet Union you've seen few signs of human life—only smoke rising here and there from the campfires of one of the nomadic tribes that roamed central Asia. But now, as you pass over more fertile regions to the west, you see signs of stable settlements: cattle grazing and crops growing in their fields.

"We have reached the ancient lands of the Russians," Chin Chin announces. "But the country is not yet unified. Each region is controlled by a different prince, and they are often squabbling and fighting with each other."

"*Chin Chin, slow down!*" You interrupt your computron because you've caught sight of thousands of horsemen charging across the plain! They are small of stature and have straight black hair, and they are heavily armed with bows and arrows. It appears they have just ridden forth from a huge encampment where hundreds of tents have been pitched alongside a fast-flowing stream. One of the tents, set on a knoll, stands out from all the rest. It is gleaming in the sunlight as if made of pure gold! Could this really be true? You'll never know for sure. You dare not land and investigate, because your job is to observe and not be observed, but you feel certain that you're looking at the golden tent of Batu Khan, the Mongol leader whose army of warriors conquered the Russian princes one by one.

At your command, the *Voyager* alters course and picks up speed. You head northeastward and fly over the small medieval town that will one day become the great city of Moscow. Then you climb swiftly through the stratosphere and into the star-studded blackness of space. Soon you and Tang will be on your way back to Turoc.

Go on to the next page.

In a wisp of time you traverse the space–time continuum. You watch eagerly through the viewports as the *Voyager* glides over the blue-green lakes of Turoc and sets down near the Chamber of Wisdom. You and Tang waste no time telling Simbar about your adventures and the Golden Horde.

The Surveyor of the Spheres listens intently. "Thanks for your good work," he says when you are through. "Russia is not the easiest country to inspect, or to live in. I'm glad you both returned alive and in good health."

"What I still don't understand," you say, "is why the answer to the riddle was so important."

"Think about it for a moment," Simbar says. "If a country has been conquered and ruled by foreigners, its people tend to be fearful that it will happen again. As you have learned, the Russians were ruled for centuries by the Mongols. For centuries more they were threatened by the armies of the Turks and Swedes. Then came the cruel invasions of Napoleon and finally Hitler."

"The Russians don't have anything to worry about now," Tang says.

"No, they don't," Simbar says, "but long ago they got in the habit of protecting themselves by heavily arming themselves and expanding their borders. That's a difficult habit to break."

"It didn't seem to make much difference that the czars were overthrown and the Communists took over," you say.

"Perhaps not," Simbar replies. "The Communist leaders have often been like the czars they overthrew. But as Tang learned, Mikhail Gorbachev, the present leader of Russia, has been carrying out surprising reforms. People there are allowed to speak out much more than in the past. They are beginning to have a say in their government. Russia is undergoing tremendous changes these days."

Having said this, Simbar waves his white furry arm above his head—a gesture that means, "May the power of Turoc be with you."

As the Surveyor of the Spheres glides from the chamber, Tang does one of his double backflips. He's rather startled when you follow it with a triple!

"How about ten shoots over the falls tomorrow?" you say.

Tang sends a thought wave: *Sounds good to me!*

The End

As the *Voyager* decelerates you spot Tang's craft, the *Ranger*, swooping into position nearby.

"Welcome to Earth," you radio; then you hear Tang's voice.

"It's even more beautiful than I'd imagined!"

You're not surprised at his reaction. No matter how many times one sees Earth from space, it's always an exciting sight.

"The Soviet Union is as big as the whole planet Vorkar," Tang radios. "How shall we know where to begin?"

"Chin Chin," you ask, "do you have any useful data for us?" You patch his voice circuit into your transmitter so Tang can hear his answer.

"Much of the country is thinly populated," Chin Chin reports in a moment. "Most people live either in western Russia or along the route of the Trans-Siberian Railroad—the longest in the world. It runs eight thousand miles from Moscow, the capital, all the way to Vladivostok on the Sea of Japan."

"I have an idea," Tang says when he hears this. "Why not have one of us start from the western end of the railroad line and the other start from the eastern end and we'll meet in the middle. One of us is bound to find the answer to the riddle on the way."

"If we did that, where would be the best place to meet?" you ask Chin Chin.

Your computron hums for a moment, then says, "I suggest Novosibirsk, a great city in Central Asia. You could meet at the statue of Lenin, the founder of the Soviet Union."

"Are you sure there's a statue of Lenin there, Chin Chin? We don't want to miss each other."

"*Every* city in Russia has a statue of Lenin," is the reply.

"Chin Chin, you must be programmed with more information than I realized," you say. "You don't happen to know what the Golden Horde is, do you?"

After hearing this, Chin Chin hums for a long time. Wouldn't it be great if he actually knew the answer! You and Tang would be back on your splash boards in no time.

But when his reply comes, it's the one you expected:

Insufficient data.

"Well, then, Tang," you say, "it's April fifteenth on Earth. Let's meet on June fifteenth. That should give us each enough time."

"That's fine with me," he says. "June fifteenth at the statue of Lenin in Novosibirsk. Where would you like to start?"

If you decide to land at the eastern end of the Trans-Siberian Railroad, turn to page 13.

If you decide to land at the western end, turn to page 16.

Your cell-mate, a gray-bearded man, looks up as the guards close the barred door behind you. He doesn't look like a criminal, but then neither do you.

"Andrei Denisov is my name," he says. "What did they lock you up for?"

"I don't know. I was walking on the street near the fishing piers and they said I have no papers. What did they mean by that?"

Andrei looks surprised. "But of course you know, don't you? All citizens are required to have passports."

"Even traveling in their own country?"

He lets out a little laugh. "Do you think you're in America or someplace like that, my friend?"

"I'm beginning to wish I was," you say. "Why are you here?"

"I publish a little magazine," Andrei says. "And I was foolish enough to print an article in which I said Lenin should have thought more about human rights."

"They locked you up for that?"

Andrei grins. "You see me sitting here before you."

"That's really outrageous," you say. "I hope they let you out soon."

"I think they will," Andrei says, "if I promise not to misbehave anymore. But what about you? Why didn't you have any papers? In most places that wouldn't be so bad, but Vladivostok is one of our most important naval bases. No foreigners are allowed to visit here. The police might have thought you were on the pier to spy on the movement of warships."

"Spy—in all that rain and fog? That's ridiculous."

"Ridiculous things happen in Russia," Andrei says. "Look behind you."

You turn in time to see a guard opening the door. He points at you. "Come with me."

Andrei gets up and rests a hand on your shoulder. "They'll probably have a KGB man talk to you. I wish you good luck."

The guard pulls you away by the arm and leads you down the hall. You're beginning to feel angry about the treatment you're getting. You didn't even get a chance to ask Andrei about the Golden Horde!

The guard shows you into a small office with cinder-block walls like the ones in your cell, except these are freshly painted. A thin-faced man in a neat, rather threadbare suit is sitting on the other side of a metal desk. Over his head is a framed picture of Vladimir Ilyich Lenin, the founder of the Soviet Union.

The man gestures for you to sit in the metal chair across the desk from him. He riffles through some papers.

"Why am—?"

He silences you with an impatient gesture. "*I* will ask the questions, comrade."

You decide not to argue.

He stares at you for almost a minute. Finally he says, "The police saw you walking on the Dobrykin pier. You have no explanation?"

You shake your head.

"Yet you're walking on a pier from which you can watch a third of the Russian fleet go by."

"It was dark and rainy. I couldn't see anything."

The KGB man nods. "You tried but did not succeed, eh?"

"I did not try!"

"Oh, I see. When you got there you decided it was too foggy to try?"

"No!"

"No? It *wasn't* too foggy for you to see? Then you lied to me when you said that it was!"

"You're twisting my words!" you shout. (You're really getting mad now.)

"You are a clever one," the man says. "You think I'll believe you're Russian because you look like a Russian and speak the language fluently. You should understand that we are trained to notice the slightest variations. There is something different about the way you talk, something that tells me you are not really Russian at all—that you are a foreign spy!" His fist crashes down on the table.

You shudder—this is beginning to get serious. And of course he's right about your not really being Russian.

"They will want to talk to you at KGB headquarters in Moscow," the man says in a softer tone of voice. "And because I am a kindly man I'm going to give you a chance. You can either go with a carload of prisoners on the Trans-Siberian Railroad—leaving for Moscow in the morning—or you can wait in jail here a few days and be taken on the next KGB plane. In either case you'll arrive at the capital in about a week. That will give you time to think over what you're going to say." He leans across the desk and wiggles a finger in your face. "Let me tell you, my friend—you better have a good story to tell when you reach Moscow, or things will go very badly for you!"

The KGB agent gives you half an hour to make your decision, and orders you returned to your cell. You're glad to find that Andrei is still there.

Your cell-mate shakes his head repeatedly as you tell him about your interrogation. "It doesn't look good for you," he says. "They aren't going to let you go until they find out what the truth is. Maybe you ought to tell me what you were doing on the pier. Then I could advise you. Of course, I can't blame you if you don't want to talk to me. This cell is probably bugged, and for all you know I'm an informer myself!"

"I'll be glad to tell you, Andrei," you say, "and I don't care if this place is bugged, and I don't think you're an informer. The truth is I'm not doing anything wrong. I came here to find the answer to the question *What is the Golden Horde?* Would you happen to know the answer?"

Andrei looks at you thoughtfully. "I'd tell you if I knew," he says, "but I don't. That phrase sounds familiar, though. I think—" Andrei stops in mid-sentence as the door flies open. It's the guard again. This time he has come for Andrei!

"Good luck," you say as the guard takes his arm.

"Good luck to you too," Andrei calls over his shoulder, and then he is gone.

A few minutes later the KGB man who questioned you glares in at you through the bars. "Well, have you reached a decision? If you haven't, I'll decide for you!"

If you say you'll wait in jail and then be flown to Moscow in the KGB plane, turn to page 27.

If you say you'll ride with other prisoners on the train leaving in the morning, turn to page 36.

Each afternoon, before you have to go to work, you return to the square in front of the Opera and Ballet Theater in hopes of seeing Tang. One afternoon you catch the eye of a young Russian standing near the statue of Lenin. There's something familiar about him—it's Tang! You'd almost forgotten that he was bioformed to look like a Russian too!

"Am I glad to see you!" you call, running up to him. "I almost didn't make it—they thought I was a spy. I found they'll put you in jail just for writing articles they don't like, or traveling without a passport."

"It's a shame you had to land back in 1975," Tang says. "Things got much better in later years. When Gorbachev became Russia's secretary general in the 1980s, he promoted a new policy called *perestroika*—they're trying to make their government more efficient and democratic. "It's really exciting! People are allowed now to criticize the government, at least to a degree. It's part of a new policy called *glasnost*—openness."

"That's good news," you say. "Do you think they will adopt something like the Bill of Rights that Americans have in their Constitution?"

Tang shrugs. "Perhaps. But from what I've seen of the world, big changes like that usually take a long time to come about."

"Tang, I'm so glad to see you, I almost forgot: Did you get any clues about the Golden Horde?"

"I don't know if you'd call them clues—I got a lot of advice," he says. "Someone told me to check out the Russian Revolution in 1917 and 1918, so I visited Moscow then and just barely got out alive!"

"What was the Russian Revolution, exactly?" you ask.

"Well, as you know," says Tang, "Russia was ruled by czars for hundreds of years. That's what they called their emperors. In 1917 the Communists, led by Lenin, took over by force. They threw the last czar, Nicholas II, out on his ear. In fact, they shot him. They almost shot me too! I had trouble convincing them that I wasn't a spy for the people trying to stop the revolution—the 'white Russians,' as they're called. I got some other tips too, which I didn't have time to follow up."

"What?"

"Someone told me that the Golden Horde could be found during the reign of Catherine the Great!"

"Well, someone told *me* that the Golden Horde could be found during the reign of Peter the Great," you say.

"Hmm. Well, either way we'll have to go back into the past," Tang says.

"So, let's go," you say.

"The *Ranger*'s right over there," Tang says. "I transformed it into that statue of a horse and rider."

You look where your friend is pointing. "That certainly is an ugly statue, Tang—I don't think anyone will hate to see it go."

He laughs. "They'll probably order another statue of Lenin to replace it."

That night—very late, when the street is almost deserted—you and Tang transform the statue back into the *Ranger*. A few minutes later you're in the air—high over Siberia. Tang flies you back to Vladivostok, where your spacecraft—still a bunch of pilings at the end of the fishermen's pier—is waiting. Soon you're back at the controls of the *Voyager*, soaring into space. The *Ranger* is flying alongside—so close you want to reach out and touch it!

"Ready for transit?" You hear Tang's voice over the radio. "I'll check out Catherine the Great."

"Ready," you answer. "I'll visit Russia during the reign of Peter the Great."

Turn to page 77.

Your trip with Sergei takes you to the city of Astrakhan, where the Volga enters the Caspian Sea. From there you travel southeastward over increasingly arid land until you arrive in Tashkent, the fourth-largest city in the Soviet Union. You are now in the heart of central Asia, only 200 miles north of the Afghanistan border. The people in this part of the Soviet Union are mostly Moslem, and many buildings have Moslem architecture. Instead of churches in each town there are mosques!

Your journey then takes you northward past 300-mile-long Lake Balkash, then through the foothills of the Altai Mountains, and finally to Novosibirsk, where Sergei lets you out in a square in front of the Opera and Ballet Theater. You thank him heartily and give him one of your precious Nutra-Max bars, and another one for him to send to Natasha. Sergei, in the Russian fashion, gives you a kiss on each cheek before wishing you good luck and bidding you farewell.

Turn to page 60.

Half an hour has passed when you hear a distant rumbling on the tracks behind you. You stop and stare down the line. There's nothing for the mile or so stretch to the bend, but the rumbling grows louder. You wade through the snow. You're about six feet away from the tracks when you see a locomotive coming around the bend. You duck down and watch through a little hole in the snow. A double diesel rig is pulling a long line of freight cars.

The train begins to pass you. It's traveling much more slowly than the passenger train you were on, and it slows even more as the locomotives begin to ascend the steep grade ahead. You watch a dozen coal cars go by, then a line of flatcars loaded with tree trunks, then four cars loaded with steel girders. The last few cars are boxcars, and by the time the last one is approaching, you've made up your mind. You lunge out of the snow and leap up and grab one of the handrails and swing aboard. You catch your breath for a moment, swinging and swaying as the car rattles over the rails, then work your way forward to a sliding steel door. Fortunately, it's not padlocked.

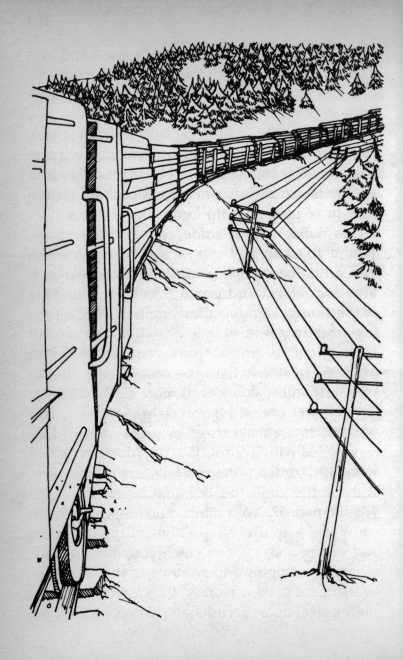

You hold onto the handrail with one hand and yank at the handle with the other. The door jerks open an inch. You yank again and it jerks open wide enough for you to squeeze through.

You swing inside the car and plunk yourself down on one of the cartons that half fill the space. They have Japanese markings on them. You guess they're electronic equipment, which the Russians may have paid for with lumber or oil.

It's a cold, miserable ride for the next two days, with nothing to eat but your last two Nutra-Max bars and nothing to drink but the icicles hanging off the roof of the boxcar. Whenever the train stops, you get ready to run again—never knowing when a guard may look into your car—but no one comes before the train reaches Novosibirsk. The moment it stops, you jump off and try to mingle with the crowd at the station. You've only gone a few feet, however, when two policemen stop you.

One of them says, "This is the crazy one—tried to escape from a prison train."

Turn to page 62.

Edward Packard is a graduate of Princeton University and Columbia Law School. In 1969, while telling bedtime stories to his children, he conceived of the idea of written stories in which the reader is the protagonist and makes choices affecting the plot, leading to multiple endings. Though his first book did not find a publisher for many years, Packard has since written over thirty others, and the interactive genre of fiction has been shown to appeal to children around the world.

Mona Conner, a freelance illustrator, graduated from the School of Visual Arts in New York City. Her illustrations can be seen on many book covers and magazines.

Barbara Carter is a freelance illustrator living in Randolph, Vermont.